COCKTAILS

& CANAPÉS

COCKTAILS

STEP BY STEP

AN
EASY
GUIDE

& CANAPÉS

GELDING STREET PRESS

CONTENTS

INTRODUCTION

WE BELIEVE MAKING COCKTAILS SHOULD BE HASSLE FREE, SO WE'VE PREPARED MORE THAN 100 CLASSIC AND CREATIVE RECIPES TO MAKE IN A FLASH!

Want to make an alcoholic or non-alcoholic pre-dinner drink but don't have time to get your head around long-winded instructions? Feel like testing the cocktail shaker you were gifted but don't have any recipe ideas? Having friends over and need some inspiration to change things up a bit? With these quick and easy recipes at your fingertips you can prepare simple, fruity, exotic, surprising or spicy cocktails for an intimate gathering or for a crowd. The recipes are divided into alcoholic and non-alcoholic, each one just as delicious as the next!

Because pre-dinner drinks are rarely served without something to nibble on, we have included more than 40 sweet and savoury recipes to delight your tastebuds and pair perfectly with your cocktails.

THE FORMULA IS SIMPLE: there are no long instructions in this book, just the essentials: add the +, follow the ⟶ and, as surely as 1 + 1 equals 2, you will work wonders with these 150 recipes. Follow the images and you'll make the recipe. Welcome to cooking step by step!

Cocktail strainer

Blender

Paring knife

Cutting board

Ice cube trays

Ice tongs

Peeler

Mixing jug

Fruit tongs

Shaker

Graduated
pourer
20–40 ml
(2/3–1¹/3 fl oz)

Strainer
spoon

Stirring spoon

Airtight jars or bottles

Citrus juicer

01 TRADITIONAL
ti punch
—

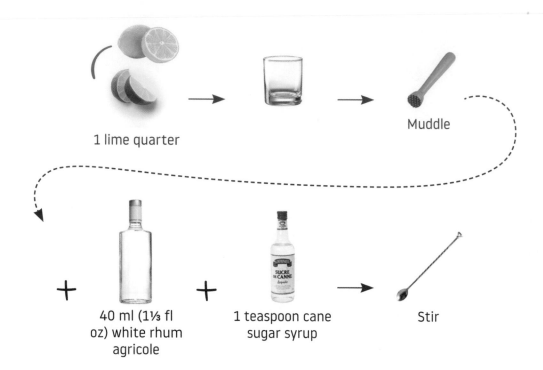

1 lime quarter

Muddle

+ 40 ml (1⅓ fl oz) white rhum agricole

+ 1 teaspoon cane sugar syrup

Stir

MAKES 1 GLASS
PREPARATION: 5 MINUTES

———————

- 1 lime quarter
- 40 ml (1⅓ fl oz) white rhum agricole
- 1 teaspoon cane sugar syrup

02 CLASSIC
caipirinha
—

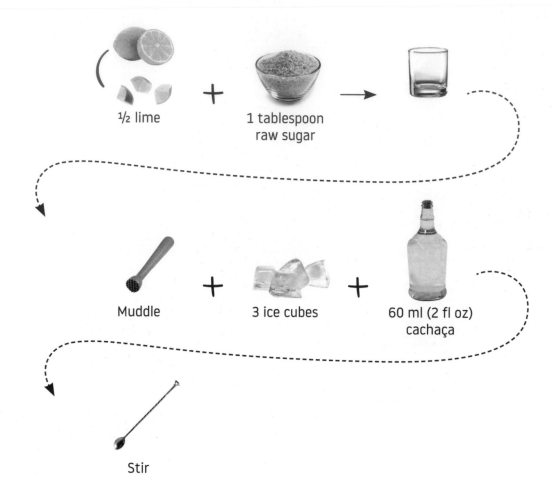

½ lime + 1 tablespoon raw sugar →

Muddle + 3 ice cubes + 60 ml (2 fl oz) cachaça

Stir

- ½ lime, diced
- 1 tablespoon raw sugar
- 3 ice cubes
- 60 ml (2 fl oz) cachaça

03 PASSIONFRUIT
caipirinha

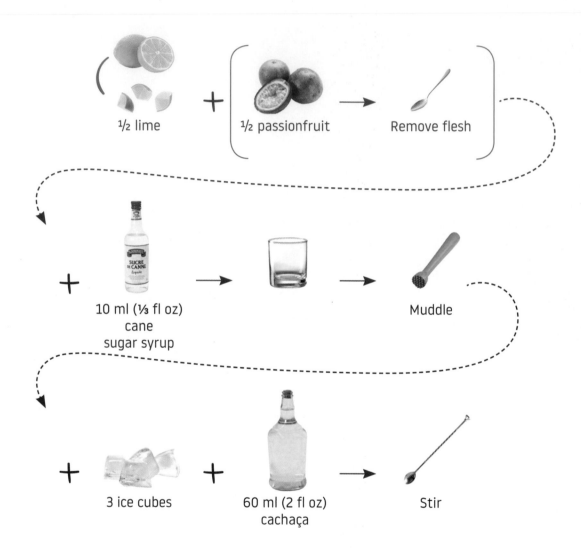

½ lime + ½ passionfruit → Remove flesh

+ 10 ml (⅓ fl oz) cane sugar syrup → [glass] → Muddle

+ 3 ice cubes + 60 ml (2 fl oz) cachaça → Stir

MAKES 1 GLASS
PREPARATION: 5 MINUTES

———————

- ½ lime, diced
- ½ passionfruit, flesh removed
- 10 ml (⅓ fl oz) cane sugar syrup
- 3 ice cubes
- 60 ml (2 fl oz) cachaça

04 CLASSIC
mojito
—

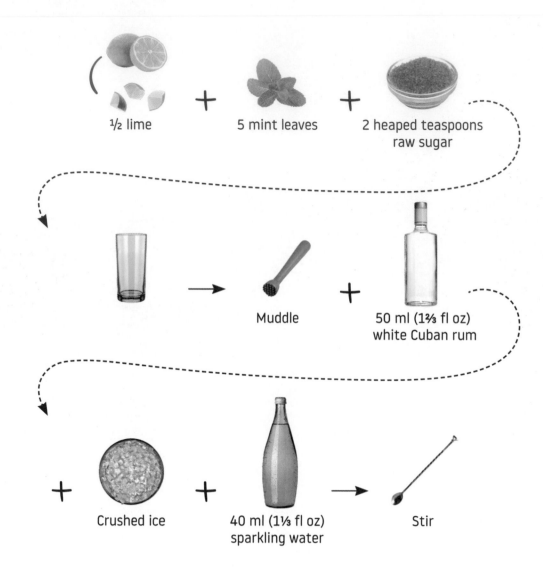

½ lime + 5 mint leaves + 2 heaped teaspoons raw sugar

Muddle + 50 ml (1⅔ fl oz) white Cuban rum

+ Crushed ice + 40 ml (1⅓ fl oz) sparkling water → Stir

MAKES 1 GLASS
PREPARATION: 5 MINUTES

_____

- ½ lime, diced
- 5 mint leaves
- 2 heaped teaspoons raw sugar
- 50 ml (1⅓ fl oz) white Cuban rum
- crushed ice
- 40 ml (1⅓ fl oz) sparkling water

05 ROSE AND RASPBERRY
mojito

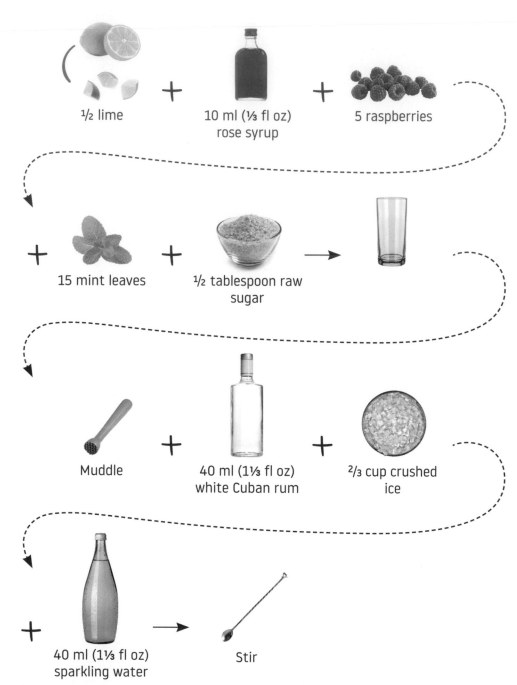

½ lime + 10 ml (⅓ fl oz) rose syrup + 5 raspberries

+ 15 mint leaves + ½ tablespoon raw sugar →

Muddle + 40 ml (1⅓ fl oz) white Cuban rum + ⅔ cup crushed ice

+ 40 ml (1⅓ fl oz) sparkling water → Stir

MAKES 1 GLASS
PREPARATION: 5 MINUTES

_____

- ½ lime, diced
- 10 ml (⅓ fl oz) rose syrup
- 5 raspberries
- 15 mint leaves
- ½ tablespoon raw sugar
- 40 ml (1⅓ fl oz) white Cuban rum
- ⅔ cup crushed ice
- 40 ml (1⅓ fl oz) sparkling water

06 CLASSIC
daiquiri

—

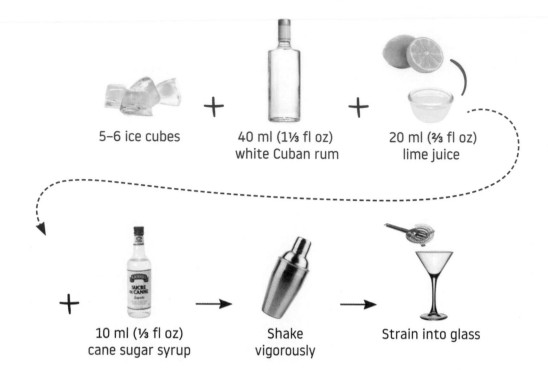

5–6 ice cubes

+

40 ml (1⅓ fl oz)
white Cuban rum

+

20 ml (⅔ fl oz)
lime juice

+

10 ml (⅓ fl oz)
cane sugar syrup

→

Shake
vigorously

→

Strain into glass

MAKES 1 GLASS
PREPARATION: 5 MINUTES

_____

- 5–6 ice cubes
- 40 ml (1⅓ fl oz) white Cuban rum
- 20 ml (⅔ fl oz) lime juice
- 10 ml (⅓ fl oz) cane sugar syrup

07 BANANA
daiquiri

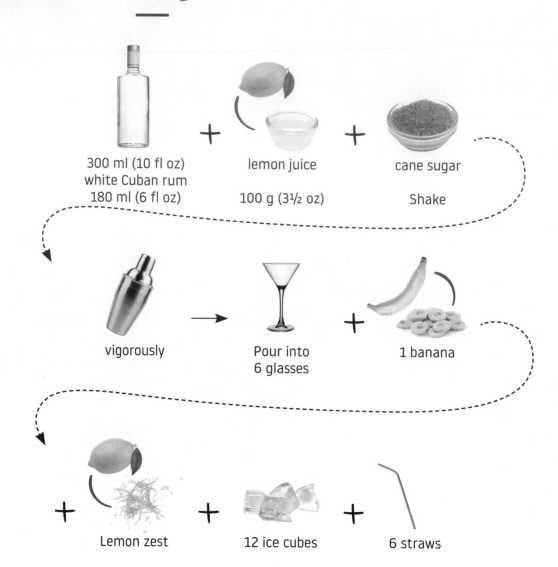

300 ml (10 fl oz)
white Cuban rum
180 ml (6 fl oz)

+

lemon juice

100 g (3½ oz)

+

cane sugar

Shake

vigorously

→ Pour into
6 glasses

+

1 banana

+

Lemon zest

+

12 ice cubes

+

6 straws

MAKES 6 GLASSES
PREPARATION: 5 MINUTES

———————

- 300 ml (10 fl oz) white Cuban rum
- 180 ml (6 fl oz) lemon juice
- 100 g (3½ oz) cane sugar
- 1 banana, sliced
- lemon zest
- 12 ice cubes

08 PLANTER'S *punch*
—

1.8 l (61 fl oz) white
rhum agricole

+

450 ml (15 fl oz) gold
rhum agricole

+

900 ml (30 fl oz)
orange juice

+

900 ml (30 fl oz)
pineapple juice

+

450 ml (15 fl oz) cane
sugar syrup

+

20 dashes
Angostura® bitters

+

20–25 ice cubes

→

Or in a large
bowl

+

1 orange

+

½ pineapple

→

Stir

MAKES 4.5 LITRES (152 FL OZ)
PREPARATION: 10 MINUTES

- 1.8 l (61 oz) white rhum agricole
- 450 ml (15 fl oz) gold rhum agricole
- 900 ml (30 fl oz) orange juice
- 900 ml (30 fl oz) pineapple juice
- 450 ml (15 fl oz) cane sugar syrup
- 20 dashes Angostura® bitters
- 20–25 ice cubes
- 1 orange, sliced
- ½ pineapple, diced

09 CUBA
libre

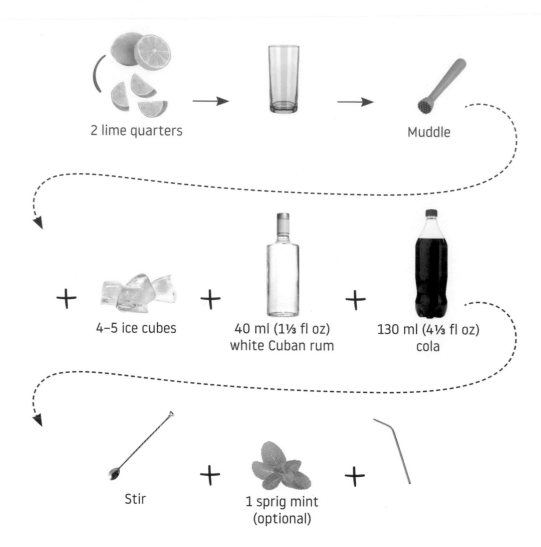

2 lime quarters → [glass] → Muddle

+ 4–5 ice cubes + 40 ml (1⅓ fl oz) white Cuban rum + 130 ml (4⅓ fl oz) cola

Stir + 1 sprig mint (optional) +

MAKES 1 GLASS
PREPARATION: 5 MINUTES

———————

- 2 lime quarters
- 4–5 ice cubes
- 40 ml (1⅓ fl oz) white Cuban rum
- 130 ml (4⅓ fl oz) cola
- 1 sprig mint (optional)

10 CLASSIC
mai tai

—

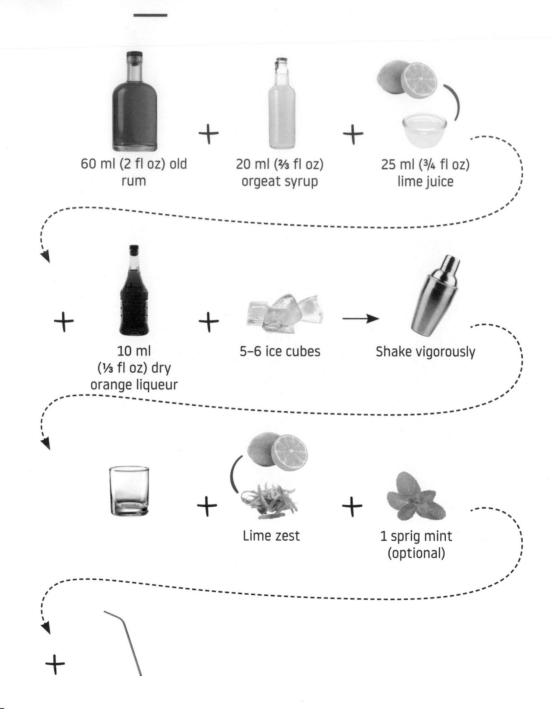

60 ml (2 fl oz) old rum

+

20 ml (⅔ fl oz) orgeat syrup

+

25 ml (¾ fl oz) lime juice

+

10 ml (⅓ fl oz) dry orange liqueur

+

5–6 ice cubes

→ Shake vigorously

Lime zest

+

1 sprig mint (optional)

+

MAKES 1 GLASS
PREPARATION: 5 MINUTES

————————

• 60 ml (2 fl oz) old rum
• 20 ml (⅔ fl oz) orgeat syrup
• 25 ml (¾ fl oz) lime juice
• 10 ml (⅓ fl oz) orange liqueur
• 5–6 ice cubes
• lime zest
• 1 sprig mint (optional)

11 PIÑA *colada*

—

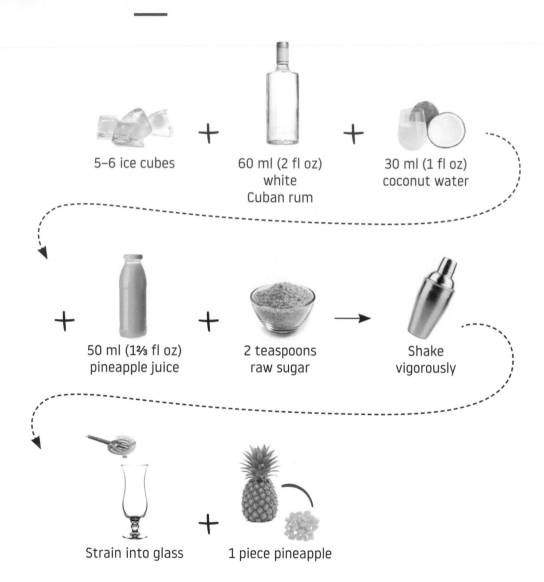

5–6 ice cubes + 60 ml (2 fl oz) white Cuban rum + 30 ml (1 fl oz) coconut water

+ 50 ml (1⅔ fl oz) pineapple juice + 2 teaspoons raw sugar → Shake vigorously

Strain into glass + 1 piece pineapple

MAKES 1 GLASS
PREPARATION: 5 MINUTES

_____

- 5–6 ice cubes
- 60 ml (2 fl oz) white Cuban rum
- 30 ml (1 fl oz) coconut water
- 50 ml (1⅔ fl oz) pineapple juice
- 2 teaspoons raw sugar
- 1 piece pineapple

12 GIANT
zombie

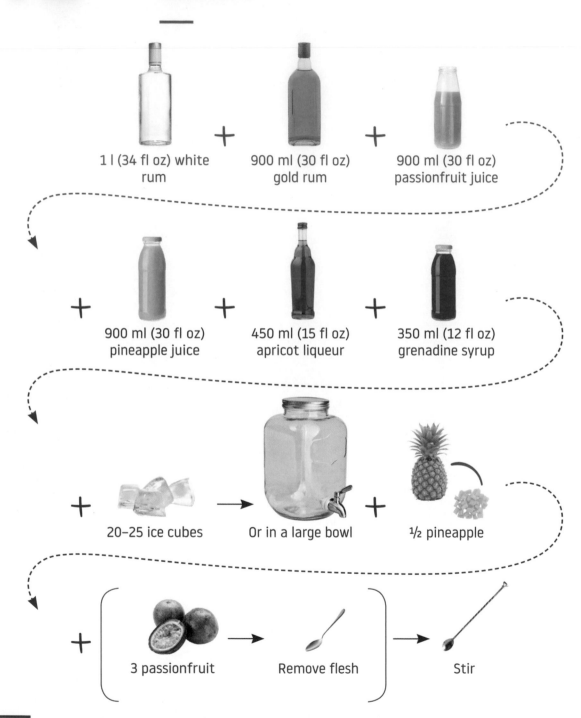

1 l (34 fl oz) white rum

+

900 ml (30 fl oz) gold rum

+

900 ml (30 fl oz) passionfruit juice

+

900 ml (30 fl oz) pineapple juice

+

450 ml (15 fl oz) apricot liqueur

+

350 ml (12 fl oz) grenadine syrup

+

20–25 ice cubes

→ Or in a large bowl

+

½ pineapple

+

3 passionfruit

→ Remove flesh

→ Stir

MAKES 4.5 LITRES (152 FL OZ)
PREPARATION: 10 MINUTES

- 1 l (34 fl oz) white rum
- 900 ml (30 fl oz) gold rum
- 900 ml (30 fl oz) passionfruit juice
- 900 ml (30 fl oz) pineapple juice
- 450 ml (15 fl oz) apricot liqueur
- 350 ml (12 fl oz) grenadine syrup
- 20–25 ice cubes
- ½ pineapple, diced
- 3 passionfruit, flesh removed

13 CUCUMBER AND JASMINE TEA
infused rum

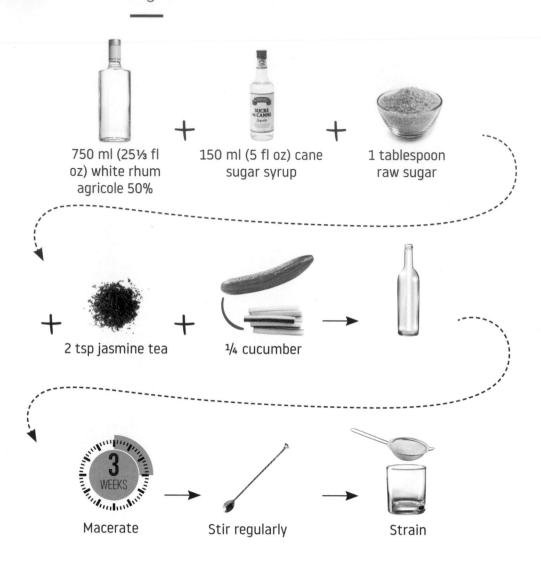

750 ml (25⅓ fl oz) white rhum agricole 50%

$+$

150 ml (5 fl oz) cane sugar syrup

$+$

1 tablespoon raw sugar

$+$

2 tsp jasmine tea

$+$

¼ cucumber

3 WEEKS — Macerate

Stir regularly

Strain

MAKES 1 LITRE (34 FL OZ)
PREPARATION: 7 MINUTES
MACERATION: 3 WEEKS

- 750 ml (25⅓ fl oz) white rhum agricole 50%
- 150 ml (5 fl oz) cane sugar syrup
- 1 tablespoon raw sugar
- 2 tsp jasmine tea
- ¼ cucumber, cut into strips

14 COPACABANA
beach

—

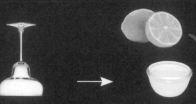 Dip rim in lime juice + Fleur de sel or sea salt

Turn the glass upright +  50 ml (1⅔ fl oz) cachaça + 20 ml (⅔ fl oz) lime juice

+ 10 ml (⅓ fl oz) cane sugar syrup + 60 ml (2 fl oz) coconut water + 1 lime slice

+  3 ice cubes → Stir

MAKES 1 GLASS
PREPARATION: 5 MINUTES

_____

- 30 ml (1 fl oz) lime juice
- fleur de sel or sea salt
- 50 ml (1⅔ fl oz) cachaça
- 10 ml (⅓ fl oz) cane sugar syrup
- 60 ml (2 fl oz) coconut water
- 1 lime slice
- 3 ice cubes

15 SMILE
pineapple, mango, passionfruit
—

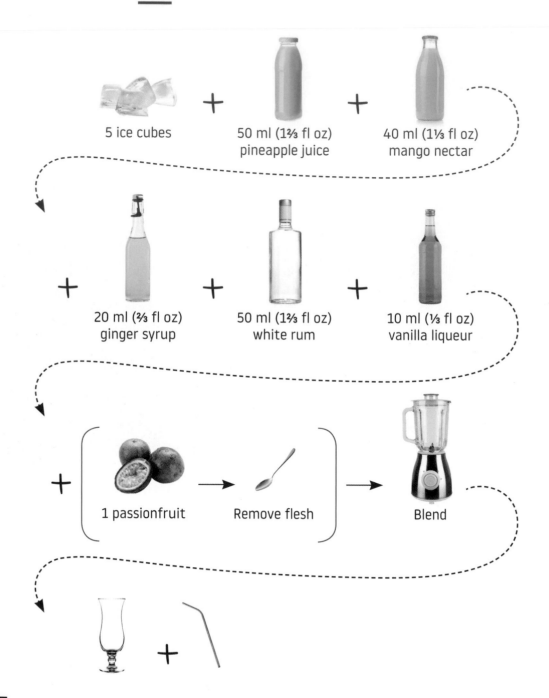

5 ice cubes + 50 ml (1⅔ fl oz) pineapple juice + 40 ml (1⅓ fl oz) mango nectar

+ 20 ml (⅔ fl oz) ginger syrup + 50 ml (1⅔ fl oz) white rum + 10 ml (⅓ fl oz) vanilla liqueur

+ [1 passionfruit → Remove flesh] → Blend

- 5 ice cubes
- 50 ml (1⅔ fl oz) pineapple juice
- 40 ml (1⅓ fl oz) mango nectar
- 20 ml (⅔ fl oz) ginger syrup
- 50 ml (1⅔ fl oz) white rum
- 10 ml (⅓ fl oz) vanilla liqueur
- 1 passionfruit, flesh removed

16 COCO
the loco

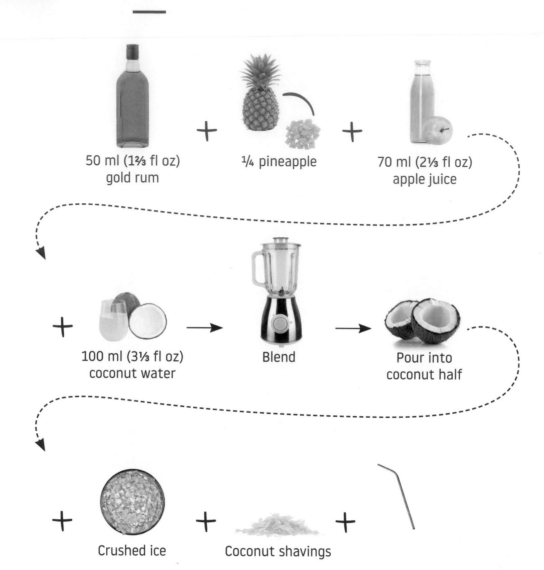

50 ml (1⅔ fl oz)
gold rum

+

¼ pineapple

+

70 ml (2⅓ fl oz)
apple juice

+

100 ml (3⅓ fl oz)
coconut water

→

Blend

→

Pour into
coconut half

+

Crushed ice

+

Coconut shavings

+

MAKES 1 GLASS
PREPARATION: 5 MINUTES

- 50 ml (1⅔ fl oz) gold rum
- ¼ pineapple, diced
- 70 ml (2⅓ fl oz) apple juice
- 100 ml (3⅓ fl oz) coconut water
- coconut half
- crushed ice
- coconut shavings

17 THE IRISH
apple, cider and beer

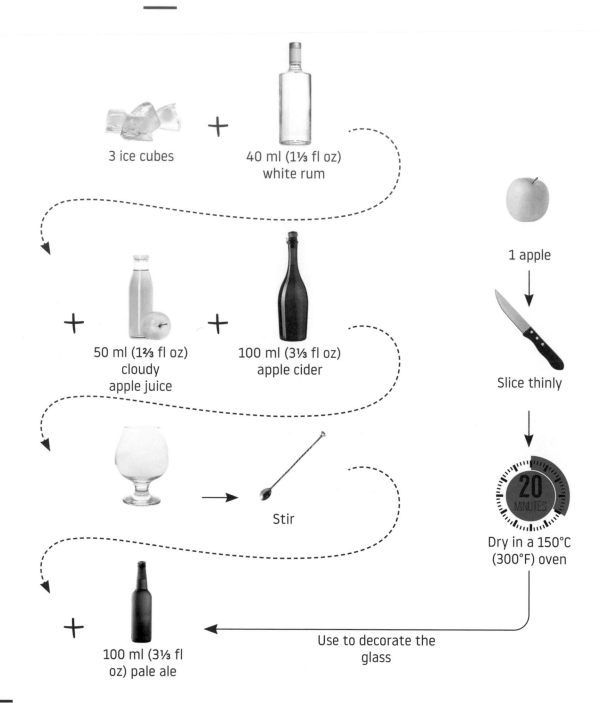

3 ice cubes + 40 ml (1⅓ fl oz) white rum

+ 50 ml (1⅔ fl oz) cloudy apple juice + 100 ml (3⅓ fl oz) apple cider

1 apple

Slice thinly

Dry in a 150°C (300°F) oven

Stir

Use to decorate the glass

+ 100 ml (3⅓ fl oz) pale ale

MAKES 1 GLASS
PREPARATION: 10 MINUTES
COOKING: 20 MINUTES

- 1 apple, thinly sliced
- 3 ice cubes
- 40 ml (1⅓ fl oz) white rum
- 50 ml (1⅔ fl oz) cloudy apple juice
- 100 ml (3⅓ fl oz) apple cider
- 100 ml (3⅓ fl oz) pale ale beer

18 CLASSIC
cosmopolitan
—

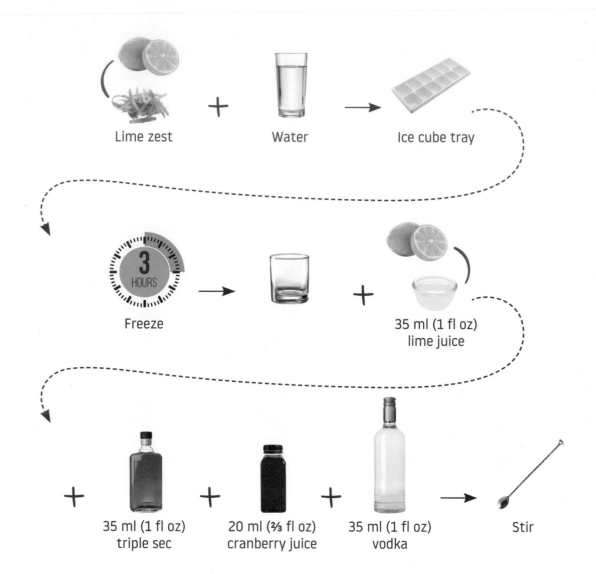

Lime zest + Water → Ice cube tray

Freeze (3 HOURS) → + 35 ml (1 fl oz) lime juice

+ 35 ml (1 fl oz) triple sec + 20 ml (⅔ fl oz) cranberry juice + 35 ml (1 fl oz) vodka → Stir

MAKES 1 GLASS
PREPARATION: 5 MINUTES
FREEZING: 3 HOURS

_____

• lime zest
• 35 ml (1 fl oz) lime juice
• 35 ml (1 fl oz) triple sec
• 20 ml (⅔ fl oz) cranberry juice
• 35 ml (1 fl oz) vodka

19 MOSCOW
mule
—

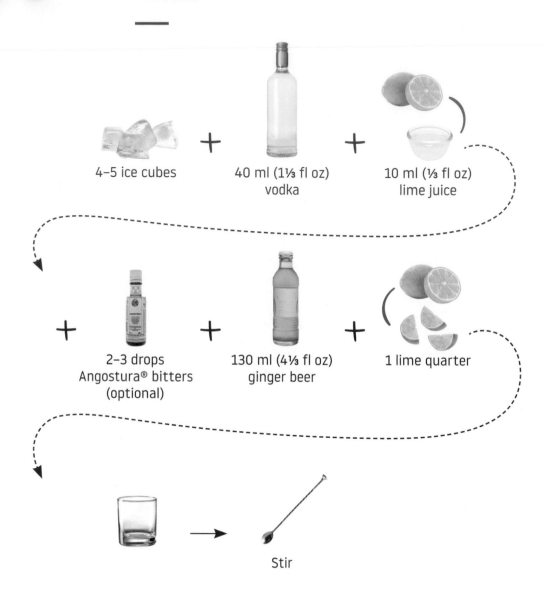

4–5 ice cubes + 40 ml (1⅓ fl oz) vodka + 10 ml (⅓ fl oz) lime juice

+ 2–3 drops Angostura® bitters (optional) + 130 ml (4⅓ fl oz) ginger beer + 1 lime quarter

→ Stir

MAKES 1 GLASS
PREPARATION: 5 MINUTES

_____

- 4–5 ice cubes
- 40 ml (1⅓ fl oz)
- vodka
- 10 ml (⅓ fl oz) lime juice
- 2–3 drops Angostura® bitters (optional)
- 130 ml (4⅓ fl oz) ginger beer
- 1 lime quarter

20 BLOODY *Mary*

—

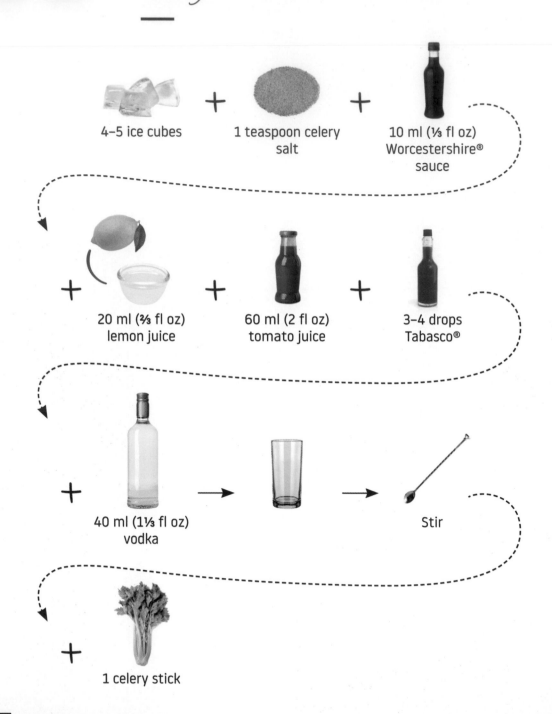

4–5 ice cubes + 1 teaspoon celery salt + 10 ml (⅓ fl oz) Worcestershire® sauce

+ 20 ml (⅔ fl oz) lemon juice + 60 ml (2 fl oz) tomato juice + 3–4 drops Tabasco®

+ 40 ml (1⅓ fl oz) vodka → → Stir

+ 1 celery stick

MAKES 1 GLASS
PREPARATION: 5 MINUTES

———————

- 4–5 ice cubes
- 1 teaspoon celery salt
- 10 ml (⅓ fl oz) Worcestershire® sauce
- 20 ml (⅔ fl oz) lemon juice
- 60 ml (2 fl oz) tomato juice
- 3–4 drops Tabasco®
- 40 ml (1⅓ fl oz) vodka
- 1 celery stick

21 LONG ISLAND
iced tea

—

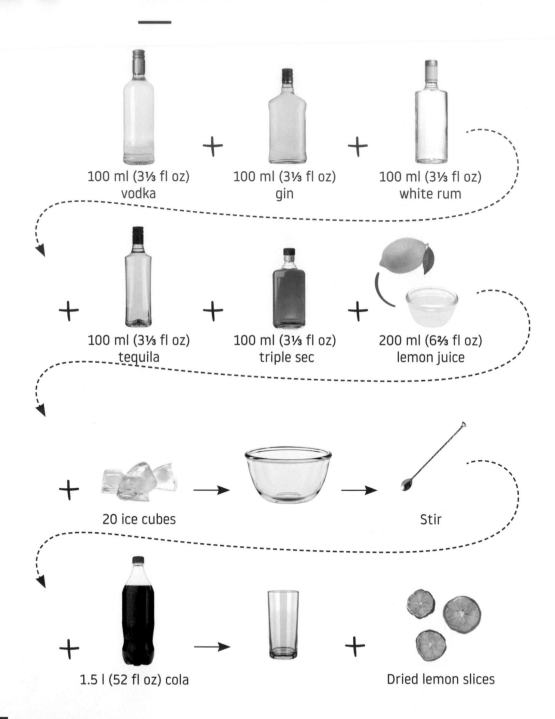

100 ml (3⅓ fl oz)
vodka

+

100 ml (3⅓ fl oz)
gin

+

100 ml (3⅓ fl oz)
white rum

+

100 ml (3⅓ fl oz)
tequila

+

100 ml (3⅓ fl oz)
triple sec

+

200 ml (6⅔ fl oz)
lemon juice

+

20 ice cubes

→

→

Stir

+

1.5 l (52 fl oz) cola

→

+

Dried lemon slices

MAKES 2.2 LITRES
(74⅓ FL OZ)
PREPARATION: 10 MINUTES

_____

- 100 ml (3⅓ fl oz) vodka
- 100 ml (3⅓ fl oz) gin
- 100 ml (3⅓ fl oz) white rum
- 100 ml (3⅓ fl oz) tequila
- 100 ml (3⅓ fl oz) triple sec
- 200 ml (6⅔ fl oz) lemon juice
- 20 ice cubes
- 1.5 l (51 fl oz) cola
- dried lemon slices

22 CLASSIC
caipiroska

—

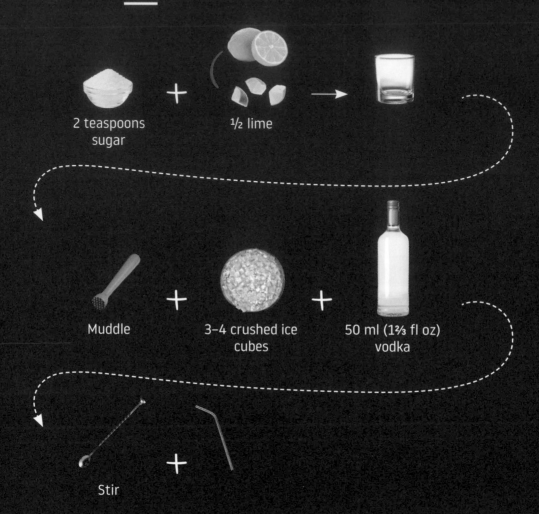

2 teaspoons sugar

+

½ lime

→

Muddle

+

3–4 crushed ice cubes

+

50 ml (1⅔ fl oz) vodka

Stir

+

MAKES 1 GLASS
PREPARATION: 5 MINUTES

———————————

• 2 teaspoons sugar
• ½ lime, diced
• 3–4 crushed ice cubes
• 50 ml (1⅔ fl oz) vodka

23

VODKA MARTINI
extra dry

—

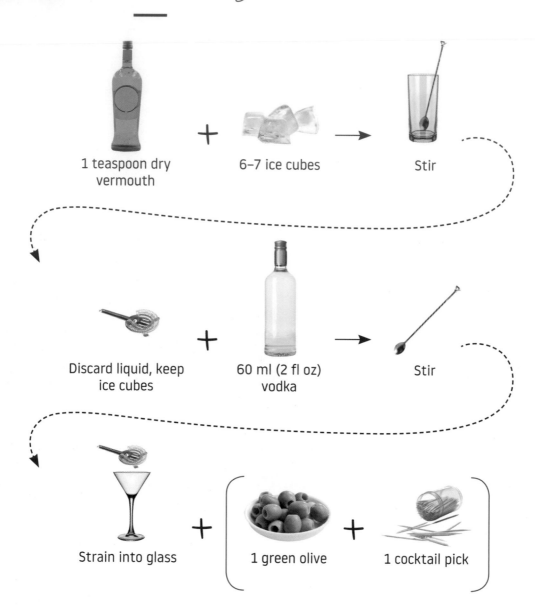

1 teaspoon dry
vermouth

6–7 ice cubes

Stir

Discard liquid, keep
ice cubes

60 ml (2 fl oz)
vodka

Stir

Strain into glass

1 green olive

1 cocktail pick

MAKES 1 GLASS
PREPARATION: 5 MINUTES

_____

- 1 teaspoon dry vermouth
- 6–7 ice cubes
- 60 ml (2 fl oz) vodka
- 1 green olive

24 SEX
on the beach

—

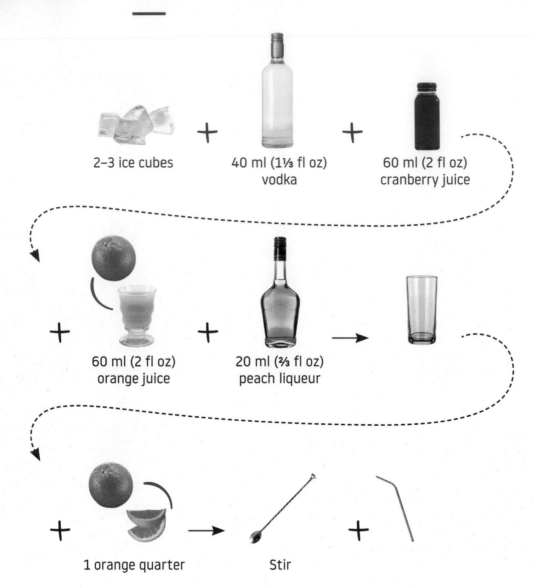

2–3 ice cubes + 40 ml (1⅓ fl oz) vodka + 60 ml (2 fl oz) cranberry juice

+ 60 ml (2 fl oz) orange juice + 20 ml (⅔ fl oz) peach liqueur →

+ 1 orange quarter → Stir +

MAKES 1 GLASS
PREPARATION: 5 MINUTES

_____

- 2–3 ice cubes
- 40 ml (1⅓ fl oz) vodka
- 60 ml (2 fl oz) cranberry juice
- 60 ml (2 fl oz) orange juice
- 20 ml (⅔ fl oz) peach liqueur
- 1 orange quarter

25 RED
passion

—

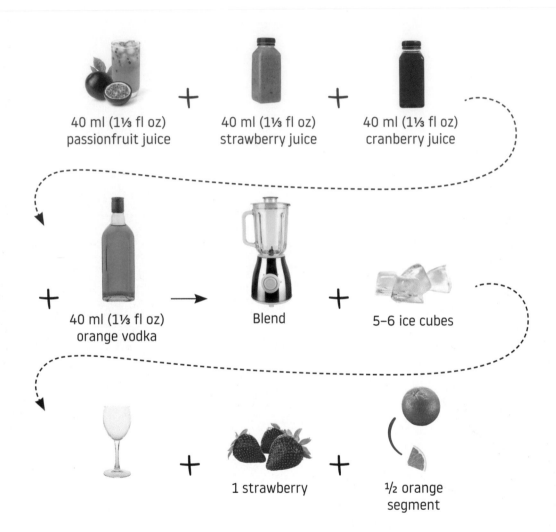

40 ml (1⅓ fl oz)
passionfruit juice

+

40 ml (1⅓ fl oz)
strawberry juice

+

40 ml (1⅓ fl oz)
cranberry juice

+

40 ml (1⅓ fl oz)
orange vodka

→ Blend

+

5–6 ice cubes

+

1 strawberry

+

½ orange
segment

MAKES 1 GLASS
PREPARATION: 5 MINUTES

- 40 ml (1⅓ fl oz) passionfruit juice
- 40 ml (1⅓ fl oz) strawberry juice
- 40 ml (1⅓ fl oz) cranberry juice
- 40 ml (1⅓ fl oz) orange vodka
- 5–6 ice cubes
- 1 strawberry
- ½ orange segment

26 BLUE *lagoon*

—

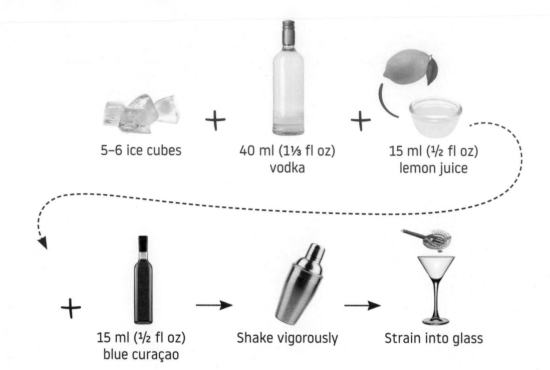

5–6 ice cubes + 40 ml (1⅓ fl oz) vodka + 15 ml (½ fl oz) lemon juice

+ 15 ml (½ fl oz) blue curaçao → Shake vigorously → Strain into glass

MAKES 1 GLASS
PREPARATION: 5 MINUTES

———————

- 5–6 ice cubes
- 40 ml (1⅓ fl oz) vodka
- 15 ml (½ fl oz) lemon juice
- 15 ml (½ fl oz) blue curaçao

27 COME *together*

1 small
watermelon

Cut in half
and flesh chopped

50 g (1¾ oz)
strawberries

4 sprigs mint

60 ml (2 fl oz)
lemon vodka

20 ml (⅔ fl oz)
lime juice

3 ice cubes

Blend

Pour into
watermelon half

MAKES 1 GLASS
PREPARATION: 5 MINUTES

––––––––––––––

• 1 small watermelon, flesh diced
• 50 g (1¾ oz) strawberries
• 4 sprigs mint
• 60 ml (2 fl oz) lemon vodka
• 20 ml (⅔ fl oz) lime juice
• 3 ice cubes

28 SPOTTED
bees

—

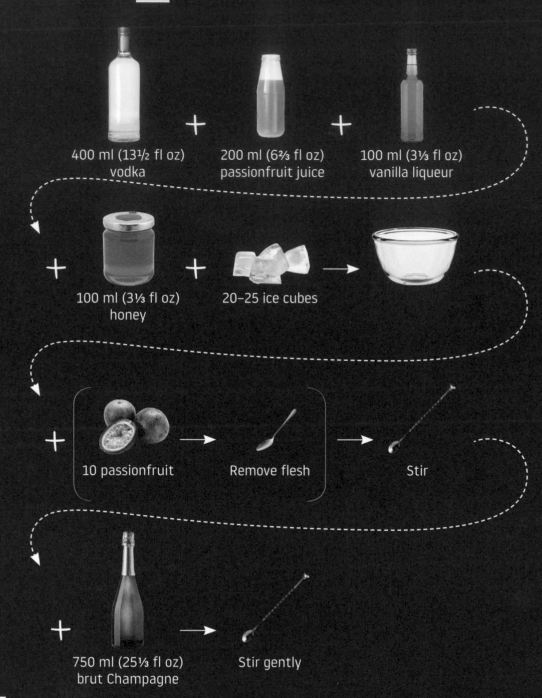

400 ml (13½ fl oz)
vodka

+

200 ml (6⅔ fl oz)
passionfruit juice

+

100 ml (3⅓ fl oz)
vanilla liqueur

+ 100 ml (3⅓ fl oz)
honey

+ 20–25 ice cubes →

+ 10 passionfruit → Remove flesh → Stir

+ 750 ml (25⅓ fl oz)
brut Champagne → Stir gently

MAKES 1.6 LITRES (54 FL OZ)
PREPARATION: 10 MINUTES

_____

- 400 ml (13½ fl oz) vodka
- 200 ml (6⅔ fl oz) passionfruit
  juice
- 100 ml (3⅓ fl oz) vanilla liqueur
- 100 ml (3⅓ fl oz) honey
- 20–25 ice cubes
- 10 passionfruit, flesh removed
- 750 ml (25⅓ fl oz) brut
  Champagne

29 PASSIONITO
peach and passionfruit
—

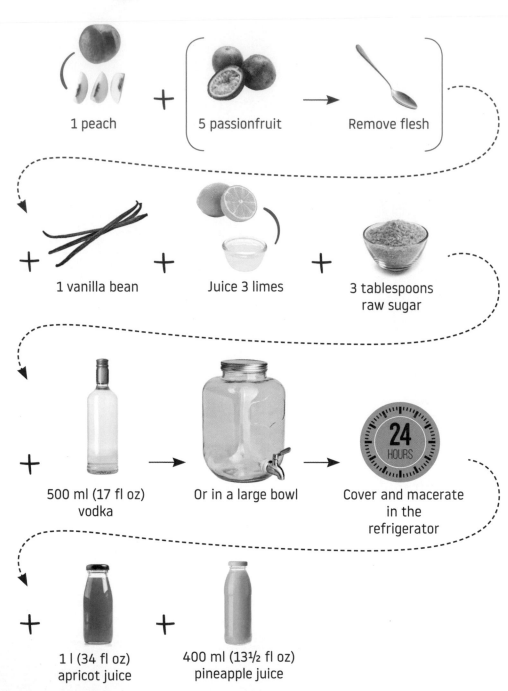

1 peach + 5 passionfruit → Remove flesh

+ 1 vanilla bean + Juice 3 limes + 3 tablespoons raw sugar

+ 500 ml (17 fl oz) vodka → Or in a large bowl → **24 HOURS** Cover and macerate in the refrigerator

+ 1 l (34 fl oz) apricot juice + 400 ml (13½ fl oz) pineapple juice

MAKES 2 LITRES (68 FL OZ)
PREPARATION: 10 MINUTES
MACERATION: 24 HOURS

- 1 peach
- 5 passionfruit, flesh removed
- 1 vanilla bean
- 3 limes, juiced
- 3 tablespoons raw sugar
- 500 ml (17 fl oz) vodka
- 1 l (34 fl oz) apricot juice
- 400 ml (13½ fl oz) pineapple
  juice

30 COFFEE
in Moscow

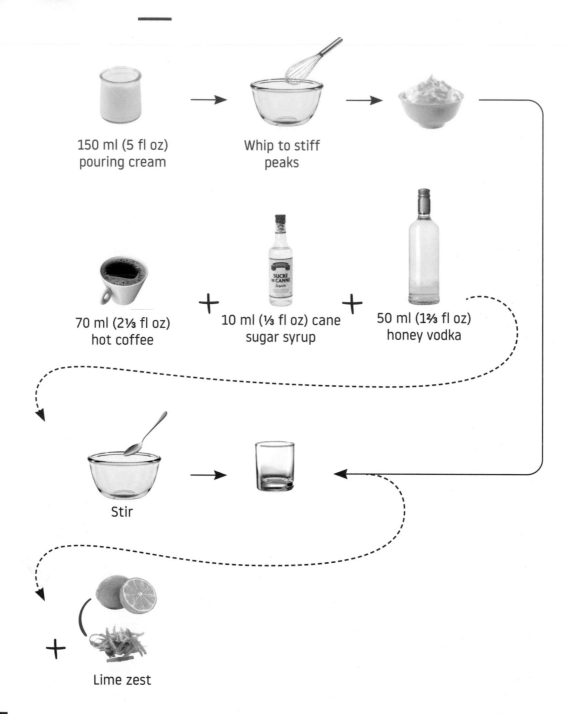

150 ml (5 fl oz)
pouring cream

Whip to stiff
peaks

70 ml (2⅓ fl oz)
hot coffee

+

10 ml (⅓ fl oz) cane
sugar syrup

+

50 ml (1⅔ fl oz)
honey vodka

Stir

+

Lime zest

MAKES 1 GLASS
PREPARATION: 5 MINUTES

———————————

- 150 ml (5 fl oz) pouring cream, whipped
- 70 ml (2⅓ fl oz) hot coffee
- 10 ml (⅓ fl oz) cane sugar syrup
- 50 ml (1⅔ fl oz) honey vodka
- lime zest

CLASSIC
margarita

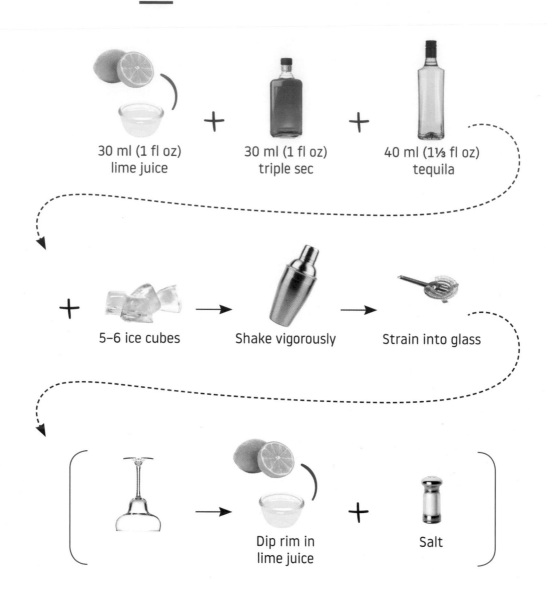

30 ml (1 fl oz)
lime juice

+

30 ml (1 fl oz)
triple sec

+

40 ml (1⅓ fl oz)
tequila

+ 5–6 ice cubes → Shake vigorously → Strain into glass

→ Dip rim in
lime juice

+ Salt

MAKES 1 GLASS
PREPARATION: 5 MINUTES

- 30 ml (1 fl oz) lime juice
- 30 ml (1 fl oz) triple sec
- 40 ml (1⅓ fl oz) tequila
- 5–6 ice cubes
- salt

32 TEQUILA
sunrise

—

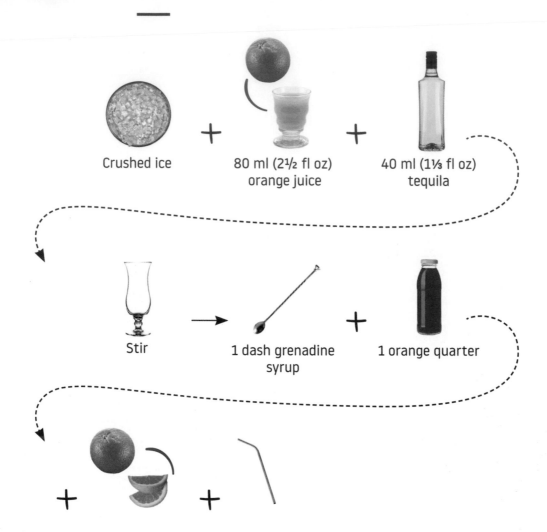

Crushed ice + 80 ml (2½ fl oz) orange juice + 40 ml (1⅓ fl oz) tequila

Stir → 1 dash grenadine syrup + 1 orange quarter

+ +

MAKES 1 GLASS
PREPARATION: 5 MINUTES
_____

- crushed ice
- 80 ml (2½ fl oz) orange juice
- 40 ml (1⅓ fl oz) tequila
- 1 dash grenadine syrup
- 1 orange quarter

33 PALOMA
grapefruit and prosecco

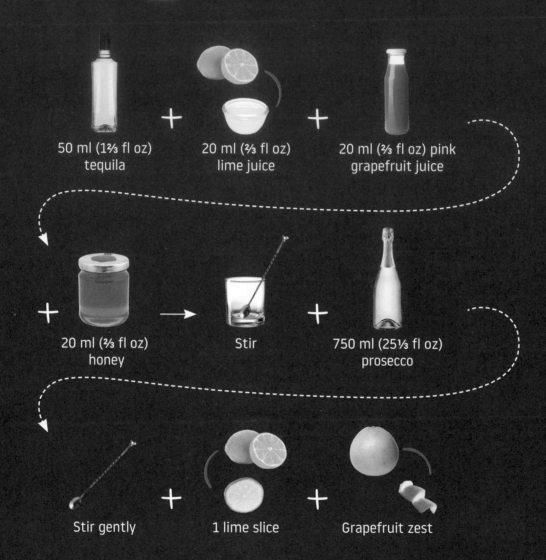

50 ml (1⅔ fl oz) tequila

+

20 ml (⅔ fl oz) lime juice

+

20 ml (⅔ fl oz) pink grapefruit juice

+

20 ml (⅔ fl oz) honey

→ Stir

+

750 ml (25⅓ fl oz) prosecco

Stir gently

+

1 lime slice

+

Grapefruit zest

MAKES 860 ML (29 FL OZ)
PREPARATION: 5 MINUTES

- 50 ml (1⅔ fl oz) tequila
- 20 ml (⅔ fl oz) lime juice
- 20 ml (⅔ fl oz) pink grapefruit juice
- 20 ml (⅔ fl oz) honey
- 750 ml (25⅓ fl oz) prosecco
- 1 lime slice
- grapefruit zest

34 MELON
cannon ball

—

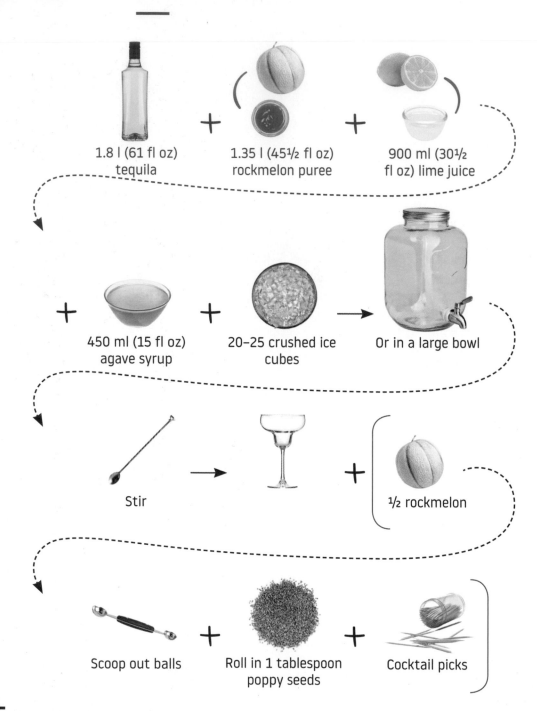

1.8 l (61 fl oz) tequila + 1.35 l (45½ fl oz) rockmelon puree + 900 ml (30½ fl oz) lime juice

+ 450 ml (15 fl oz) agave syrup + 20–25 crushed ice cubes → Or in a large bowl

Stir → + ½ rockmelon

Scoop out balls + Roll in 1 tablespoon poppy seeds + Cocktail picks

MAKES 4.5 LITRES (152 FL OZ)
PREPARATION: 10 MINUTES

_____

- 1.8 l (61 fl oz) tequila
- 1.35 l (45½ fl oz) rockmelon puree
- 900 ml (30½ fl oz) lime juice
- 450 ml (15 fl oz) agave syrup
- 20–25 crushed ice cubes
- ½ rockmelon, flesh balled
- 1 tablespoon poppy seeds

35 RUBY
blood orange and pomegranate

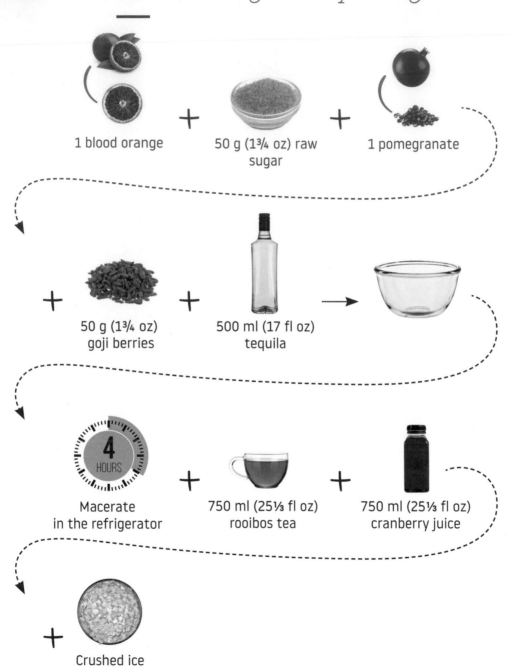

1 blood orange + 50 g (1¾ oz) raw sugar + 1 pomegranate

+ 50 g (1¾ oz) goji berries + 500 ml (17 fl oz) tequila →

4 HOURS Macerate in the refrigerator + 750 ml (25⅓ fl oz) rooibos tea + 750 ml (25⅓ fl oz) cranberry juice

+ Crushed ice

MAKES 2 LITRES (68 FL OZ)
PREPARATION: 10 MINUTES
MACERATION: 4 HOURS

- 1 blood orange, sliced
- 50 g (1¾ oz) raw sugar
- 1 pomegranate, seeded
- 50 g (1¾ oz) goji berries
- 500 ml (17 fl oz) tequila
- 750 ml (25⅓ fl oz) rooibos tea
- 750 ml (25⅓ fl oz) cranberry juice
- crushed ice

36 MANGO *flower*

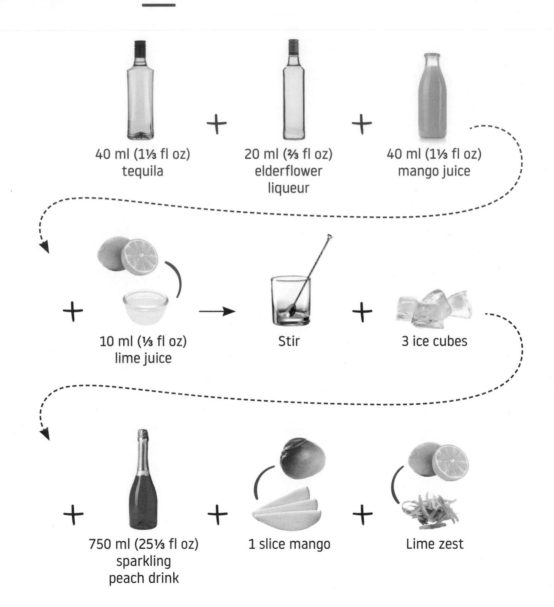

40 ml (1⅓ fl oz)
tequila

+

20 ml (⅔ fl oz)
elderflower
liqueur

+

40 ml (1⅓ fl oz)
mango juice

+

10 ml (⅓ fl oz)
lime juice

→

Stir

+

3 ice cubes

+

750 ml (25⅓ fl oz)
sparkling
peach drink

+

1 slice mango

+

Lime zest

MAKES 860 ML (29 FL OZ)
PREPARATION: 5 MINUTES

———————————

- 40 ml (1⅓ fl oz) tequila
- 20 ml (⅔ fl oz) elderflower liqueur
- 40 ml (1⅓ fl oz) mango juice
- 10 ml (⅓ fl oz) lime juice
- 3 ice cubes
- 750 ml (25⅓ fl oz) sparkling peach drink
- 1 slice mango
- lime zest

37 SECOND
chance

—

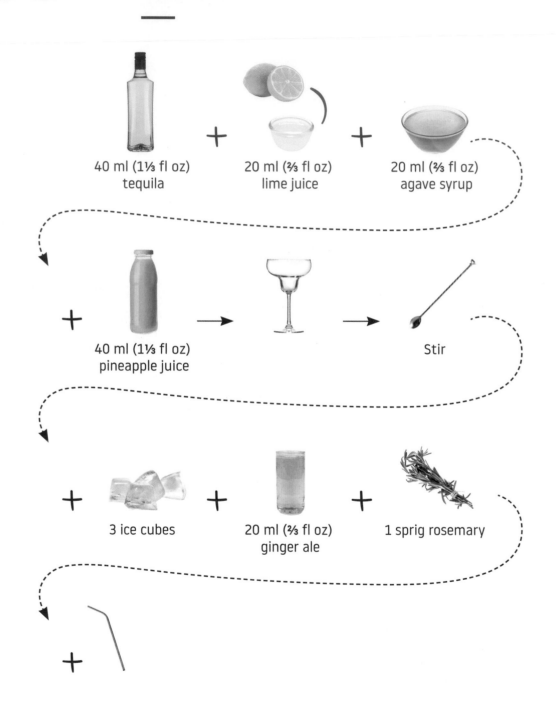

40 ml (1⅓ fl oz)
tequila

+

20 ml (⅔ fl oz)
lime juice

+

20 ml (⅔ fl oz)
agave syrup

+

40 ml (1⅓ fl oz)
pineapple juice

→

→

Stir

+

3 ice cubes

+

20 ml (⅔ fl oz)
ginger ale

+

1 sprig rosemary

+

MAKES 1 GLASS
PREPARATION: 5 MINUTES

- 40 ml (1⅓ fl oz) tequila
- 20 ml (⅔ fl oz) lime juice
- 20 ml (⅔ fl oz) agave syrup
- 40 ml (1⅓ fl oz) pineapple juice
- 3 ice cubes
- 20 ml (⅔ fl oz) ginger ale
- 1 sprig rosemary

38 BLACKCURRANT
mule

—

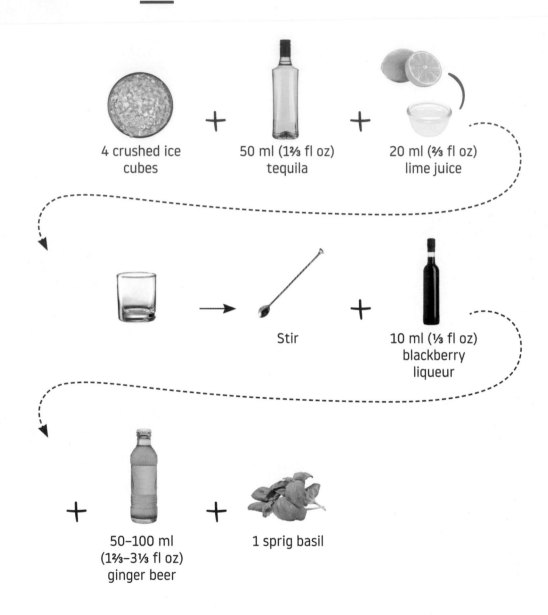

4 crushed ice
cubes

+

50 ml (1⅔ fl oz)
tequila

+

20 ml (⅔ fl oz)
lime juice

Stir

+

10 ml (⅓ fl oz)
blackberry
liqueur

+

50–100 ml
(1⅔–3⅓ fl oz)
ginger beer

+

1 sprig basil

MAKES 1 GLASS
PREPARATION: 5 MINUTES

_____

- 4 crushed ice cubes
- 50 ml (1⅔ fl oz) tequila
- 20 ml (⅔ fl oz) lime juice
- 10 ml (⅓ fl oz) blackberry liqueur
- 50–100 ml (1⅔–3⅓ fl oz) ginger beer
- 1 sprig basil

39 ORANGE
and Campari® negroni

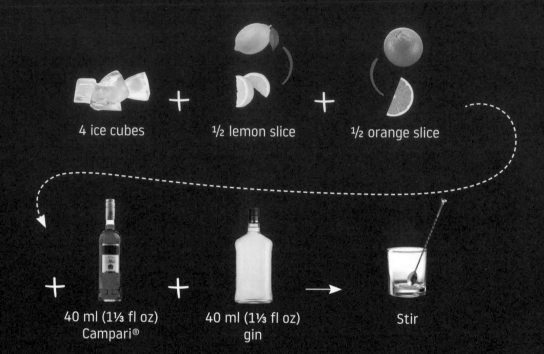

4 ice cubes + ½ lemon slice + ½ orange slice

+ 40 ml (1⅓ fl oz) Campari® + 40 ml (1⅓ fl oz) gin → Stir

MAKES 1 GLASS
PREPARATION: 5 MINUTES

- 4 ice cubes
- ½ lemon slice
- ½ orange slice
- 40 ml (1⅓ fl oz) Campari®
- 40 ml (1⅓ fl oz) gin

40 GIN
fizz

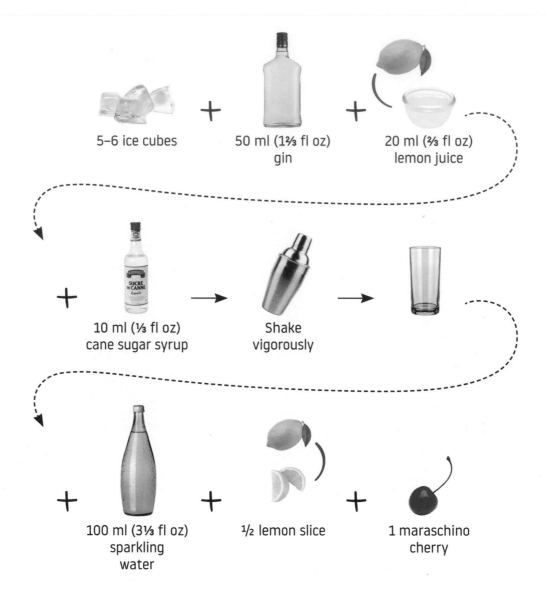

5–6 ice cubes + 50 ml (1⅔ fl oz) gin + 20 ml (⅔ fl oz) lemon juice

+ 10 ml (⅓ fl oz) cane sugar syrup → Shake vigorously →

+ 100 ml (3⅓ fl oz) sparkling water + ½ lemon slice + 1 maraschino cherry

MAKES 1 GLASS
PREPARATION: 5 MINUTE

_____

- 5–6 ice cubes
- 50 ml (1⅔ fl oz) gin
- 20 ml (⅔ fl oz) lemon juice
- 10 ml (⅓ fl oz) cane sugar syrup
- 100 ml (3⅓ fl oz) sparkling water
- ½ lemon slice
- 1 maraschino cherry

41 DRY *martini*

—

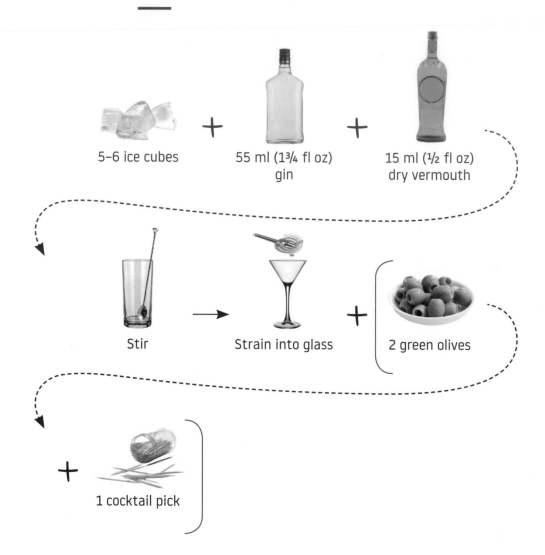

5–6 ice cubes + 55 ml (1¾ fl oz) gin + 15 ml (½ fl oz) dry vermouth

Stir → Strain into glass + 2 green olives

+ 1 cocktail pick

MAKES 1 GLASS
PREPARATION: 5 MINUTES

_____

• 5–6 ice cubes
• 55 ml (1¾ fl oz) gin
• 15 ml (½ fl oz) dry vermouth
• 2 green olives

42 ASTORIA
martini
—

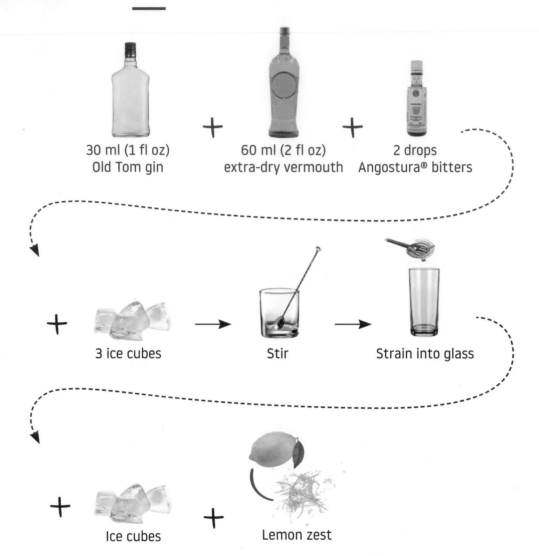

30 ml (1 fl oz)
Old Tom gin

+

60 ml (2 fl oz)
extra-dry vermouth

+

2 drops
Angostura® bitters

+ 3 ice cubes → Stir → Strain into glass

+ Ice cubes + Lemon zest

- 30 ml (1 fl oz) Old Tom gin
- 60 ml (2 fl oz) extra-dry vermouth
- 2 drops Angostura® bitters
- ice cubes
- lemon zest

43

O PICANTE
beer and chilli

—

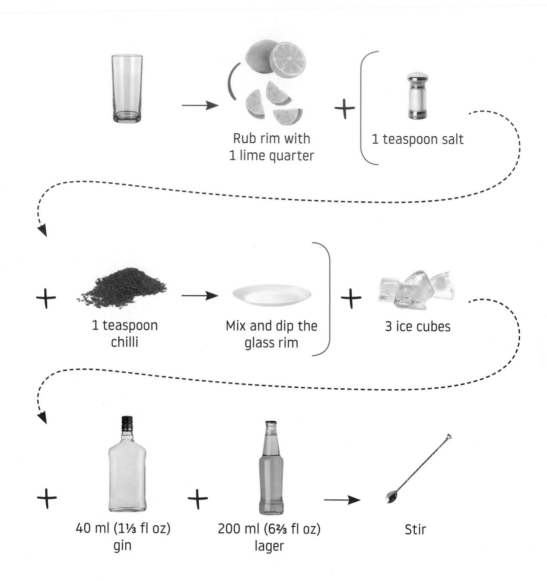

Rub rim with
1 lime quarter

+

1 teaspoon salt

+

1 teaspoon
chilli

Mix and dip the
glass rim

+

3 ice cubes

+

40 ml (1⅓ fl oz)
gin

+

200 ml (6⅔ fl oz)
lager

Stir

MAKES 1 GLASS
PREPARATION: 5 MINUTES

- 1 lime quarter
- 1 teaspoon salt
- 1 teaspoon chilli
- 3 ice cubes
- 40 ml (1⅓ fl oz) gin
- 200 ml (6⅔ fl oz) lager

44 CRANBERRY
smash

—

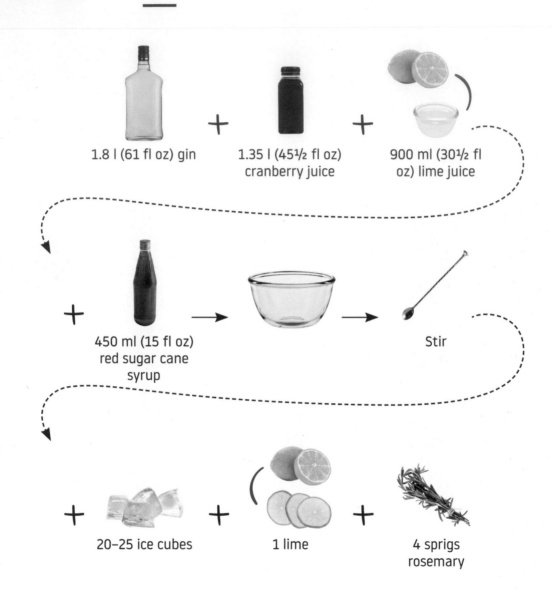

1.8 l (61 fl oz) gin

+

1.35 l (45½ fl oz) cranberry juice

+

900 ml (30½ fl oz) lime juice

+

450 ml (15 fl oz) red sugar cane syrup

→

→ Stir

+

20–25 ice cubes

+

1 lime

+

4 sprigs rosemary

MAKES 4.5 LITRES (152 FL OZ)
PREPARATION: 10 MINUTES

• 1.8 l (61 fl oz) gin
• 1.35 l (45½ fl oz) cranberry
  juice
• 900 ml (30½ fl oz) lime juice
• 450 ml (15 fl oz) red sugar
  cane syrup
• 20–25 ice cubes
• 1 lime, sliced
• 4 sprigs rosemary

45 RESURRECTION
rose syrup and wheat beer
—

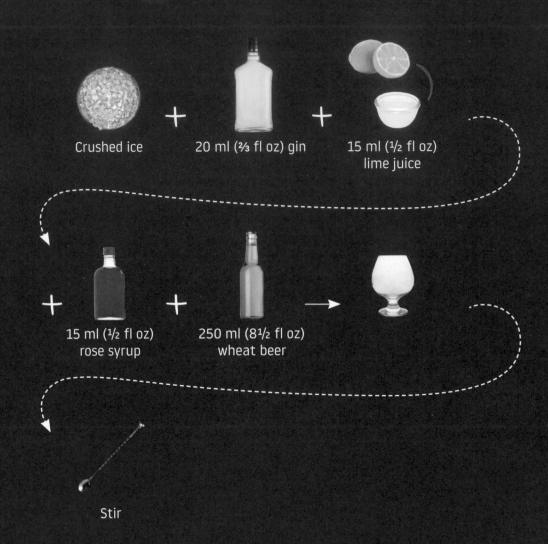

Crushed ice   +   20 ml (⅔ fl oz) gin   +   15 ml (½ fl oz) lime juice

+   15 ml (½ fl oz) rose syrup   +   250 ml (8½ fl oz) wheat beer   →

Stir

MAKES 1 GLASS
PREPARATION: 5 MINUTES

_____

- crushed ice
- 20 ml (⅔ fl oz) gin
- 15 ml (½ fl oz) lime juice
- 15 ml (½ fl oz) rose syrup
- 250 ml (8½ fl oz) wheat beer

46 GOLD
tonic
—

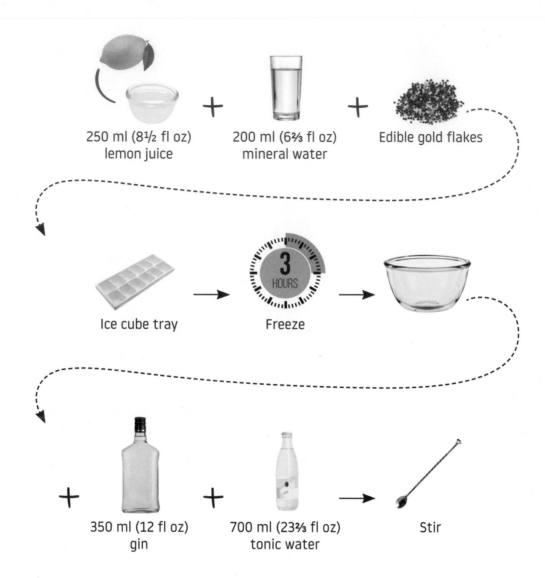

250 ml (8½ fl oz)
lemon juice

+

200 ml (6⅔ fl oz)
mineral water

+

Edible gold flakes

Ice cube tray

→

3 HOURS

Freeze

→

+

350 ml (12 fl oz)
gin

+

700 ml (23⅔ fl oz)
tonic water

→

Stir

MAKES 1.5 LITRES (51 FL OZ)
PREPARATION: 10 MINUTES
FREEZING: 3 HOURS

_____

• 250 ml (8½ fl oz) lemon juice
• 200 ml (6⅔ fl oz) mineral water
• edible gold flakes
• 350 ml (12 fl oz) gin
• 700 ml (23⅓ fl oz) tonic water

47

FRESH
air

—

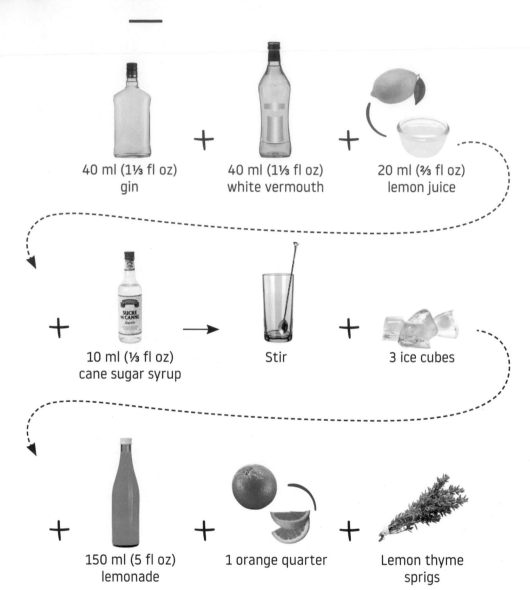

40 ml (1⅓ fl oz)
gin

+

40 ml (1⅓ fl oz)
white vermouth

+

20 ml (⅔ fl oz)
lemon juice

+

10 ml (⅓ fl oz)
cane sugar syrup

→ Stir

+

3 ice cubes

+

150 ml (5 fl oz)
lemonade

+

1 orange quarter

+

Lemon thyme
sprigs

MAKES 1 GLASS
PREPARATION: 5 MINUTES

• 40 ml (1⅓ fl oz) gin
• 40 ml (1⅓ fl oz) white
  vermouth
• 20 ml (⅔ fl oz) lemon juice
• 10 ml (⅓ fl oz) cane sugar syrup
• 3 ice cubes
• 150 ml (5 fl oz) lemonade
• 1 orange quarter
• lemon thyme sprigs

48 SÃO
Leopoldo
—

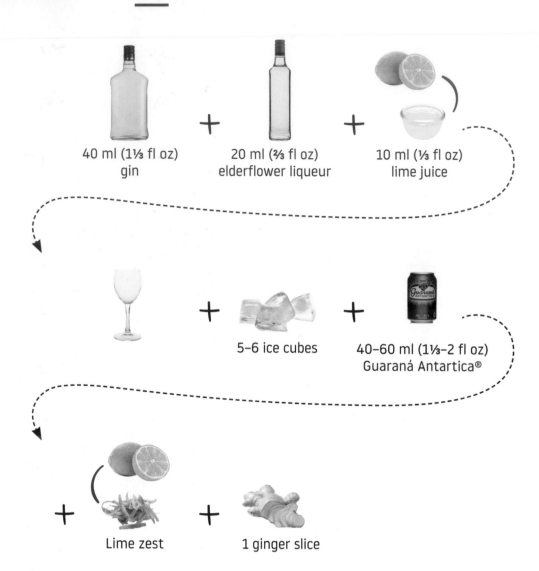

40 ml (1⅓ fl oz)
gin

+

20 ml (⅔ fl oz)
elderflower liqueur

+

10 ml (⅓ fl oz)
lime juice

+

5–6 ice cubes

+

40–60 ml (1⅓–2 fl oz)
Guaraná Antartica®

+

Lime zest

+

1 ginger slice

MAKES 1 GLASS
PREPARATION: 5 MINUTES
──────────

- 40 ml (1⅓ fl oz) gin
- 20 ml (⅔ fl oz) elderflower liqueur
- 10 ml (⅓ fl oz) lime juice
- 5–6 ice cubes
- 40–60 ml (1⅓–2 fl oz) Guaraná Antartica®
- lime zest
- 1 ginger slice

49 PARIS
punch

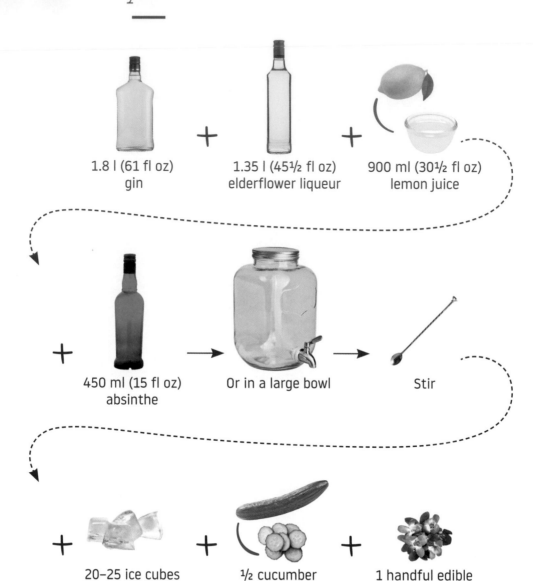

1.8 l (61 fl oz)
gin

+

1.35 l (45½ fl oz)
elderflower liqueur

+

900 ml (30½ fl oz)
lemon juice

+

450 ml (15 fl oz)
absinthe

→ Or in a large bowl → Stir

+

20–25 ice cubes

+

½ cucumber

+

1 handful edible
flowers

MAKES 4.5 LITRES (152 FL OZ)
PREPARATION: 10 MINUTES

———————

- 1.8 l (61 fl oz) gin
- 1.35 l (45½ fl oz) elderflower
  liqueur
- 900 (30½ fl oz) lemon juice
- 450 ml (15 fl oz) absinthe
- 20–25 ice cubes
- ½ cucumber, sliced
- 1 handful edible flowers

50 GIANT
manhattan

—

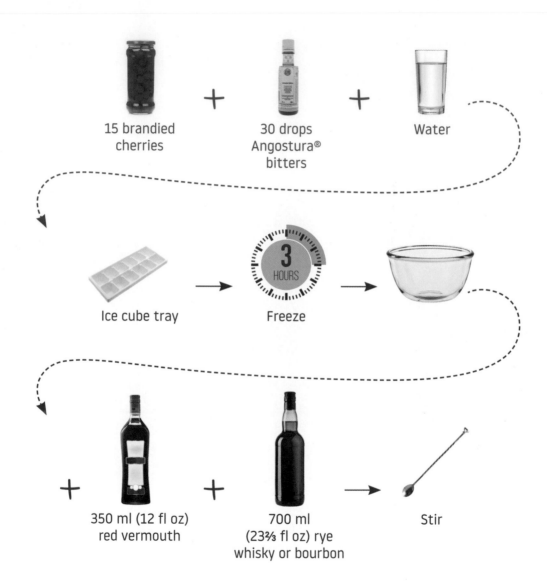

15 brandied
cherries

+

30 drops
Angostura®
bitters

+

Water

Ice cube tray

Freeze

3 HOURS

+

350 ml (12 fl oz)
red vermouth

+

700 ml
(23⅔ fl oz) rye
whisky or bourbon

Stir

MAKES 1.1 LITRES (37 FL OZ)
PREPARATION: 10 MINUTES
FREEZING: 3 HOURS

- 15 brandied cherries
- 30 drops Angostura® bitters
- 350 ml (12 fl oz) red vermouth
- 700 ml (23⅔ fl oz) rye whisky
  or bourbon

51 IRISH
coffee

300 ml (10 fl oz) Irish whisky

100 ml (3⅓ fl oz) cane sugar syrup

Heat on low

6 glasses

Gently pour 6 hot coffees

Chantilly cream

Cocoa powder

MAKES 6 GLASSES
PREPARATION: 5 MINUTES
COOKING: 3 MINUTES

- 300 ml (10 fl oz) Irish whisky
- 100 ml (3⅓ fl oz) cane sugar syrup
- 6 hot coffees
- Chantilly cream
- cocoa powder

52 CLASSIC
old fashioned
—

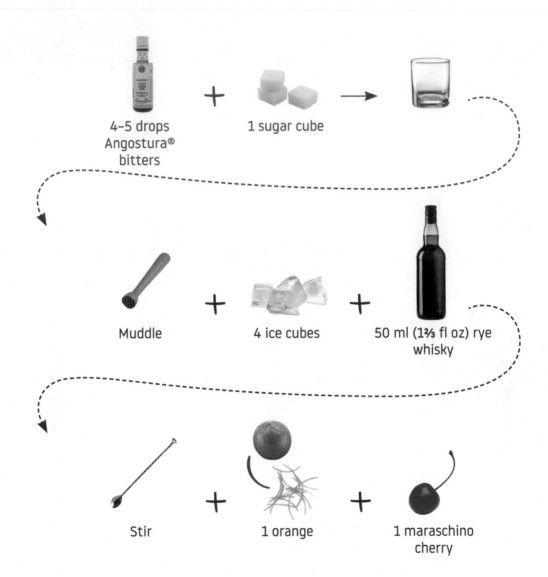

4–5 drops
Angostura®
bitters

+

1 sugar cube

→

Muddle

+

4 ice cubes

+

50 ml (1⅔ fl oz) rye
whisky

Stir

+

1 orange

+

1 maraschino
cherry

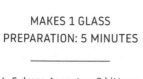

MAKES 1 GLASS
PREPARATION: 5 MINUTES

———————————

- 4–5 drops Angostura® bitters
- 1 sugar cube
- 4 ice cubes
- 50 ml (1⅔ fl oz) rye whisky
- 1 orange, lightly squeezed and zested
- 1 maraschino cherry

53 OLD *flame*

30 ml (1 fl oz)
Irish whisky

+

10 ml (⅓ fl oz)
cane sugar syrup

+

20 ml (⅔ fl oz)
red vermouth

+

3 drops
Suze Bitters®
Red Aromatic

+ Crushed ice → Shake
vigorously → + Lemon zest

+ 1 sprig rosemary → Ignite
the tip

MAKES 1 GLASS
PREPARATION: 5 MINUTES

————————————

- 30 ml (1 fl oz) Irish whisky
- 10 ml (⅓ fl oz) cane sugar syrup
- 20 ml (⅔ fl oz) red vermouth
- 3 drops Suze Bitters®
  Red Aromatic
- crushed ice
- lemon zest
- 1 sprig rosemary

54 PINEAPPLE MASH
sour

—

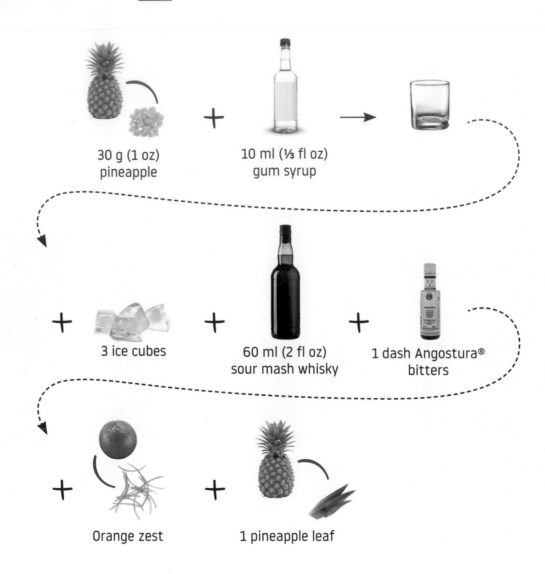

30 g (1 oz)
pineapple

+

10 ml (⅓ fl oz)
gum syrup

→

+

3 ice cubes

+

60 ml (2 fl oz)
sour mash whisky

+

1 dash Angostura®
bitters

+

Orange zest

+

1 pineapple leaf

MAKES 1 GLASS
PREPARATION: 5 MINUTES

_____

- 30 g (1 oz) pineapple, diced
- 10 ml (⅓ fl oz) gum syrup (or cane sugar syrup)
- 3 ice cubes
- 60 ml (2 fl oz) sour mash whisky
- 1 dash Angostura® bitters
- orange zest
- 1 pineapple leaf

55 OLD FASHIONED
with gingerbread syrup

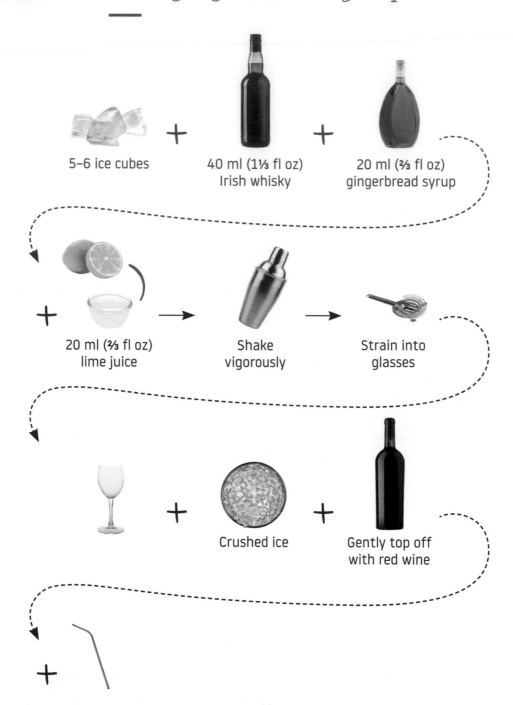

5–6 ice cubes

+

40 ml (1⅓ fl oz)
Irish whisky

+

20 ml (⅔ fl oz)
gingerbread syrup

+

20 ml (⅔ fl oz)
lime juice

→

Shake
vigorously

→

Strain into
glasses

+

Crushed ice

+

Gently top off
with red wine

+

MAKES 1 GLASS
PREPARATION: 5 MINUTES

———————

- 5–6 ice cubes
- 40 ml (1⅓ fl oz) Irish whisky
- 20 ml (⅔ fl oz) gingerbread syrup
- 20 ml (⅔ fl oz) lime juice
- crushed ice
- red wine

56 HOLIDAY
punch
—

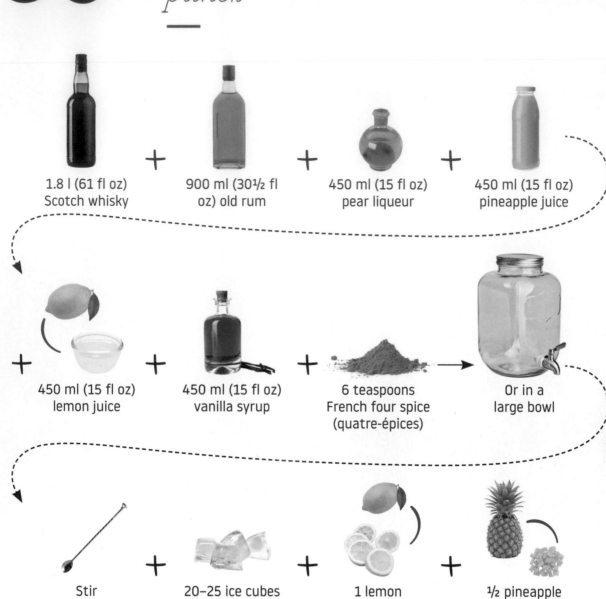

1.8 l (61 fl oz)
Scotch whisky

+

900 ml (30½ fl
oz) old rum

+

450 ml (15 fl oz)
pear liqueur

+

450 ml (15 fl oz)
pineapple juice

+

450 ml (15 fl oz)
lemon juice

+

450 ml (15 fl oz)
vanilla syrup

+

6 teaspoons
French four spice
(quatre-épices)

Or in a
large bowl

Stir

+

20–25 ice cubes

+

1 lemon

+

½ pineapple

MAKES 4.5 LITRES (152 FL OZ)
PREPARATION: 10 MINUTES

- 1.8 l (61 fl oz) Scotch whisky
- 900 ml (30½ fl oz) old rum
- 450 ml (15 fl oz) pear liqueur
- 450 ml (15 fl oz) pineapple juice
- 450 ml (15 fl oz) lemon juice
- 450 ml (15 fl oz) vanilla syrup
- 6 teaspoons French four spice
  (quatre-épices)
- 20–25 ice cubes
- 1 lemon, sliced
- ½ pineapple, diced

57 AMERICAN
mojito

—

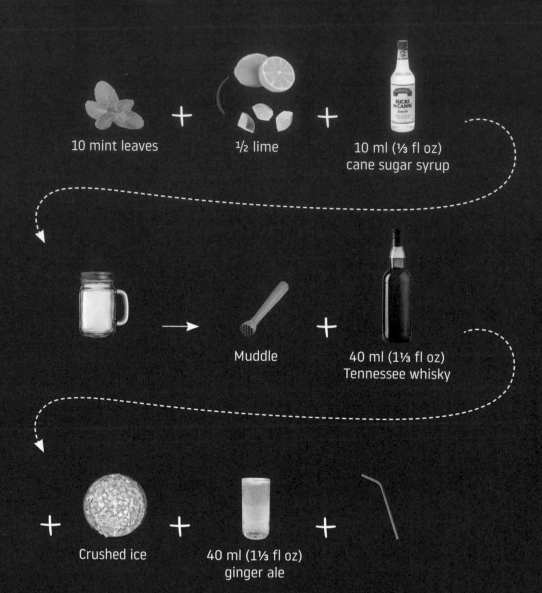

10 mint leaves + ½ lime + 10 ml (⅓ fl oz) cane sugar syrup

Muddle + 40 ml (1⅓ fl oz) Tennessee whisky

+ Crushed ice + 40 ml (1⅓ fl oz) ginger ale +

MAKES 1 GLASS
PREPARATION: 5 MINUTES

- 10 mint leaves
- ½ lime, diced
- 10 ml (⅓ fl oz) cane sugar syrup
- 40 ml (1⅓ fl oz) Tennessee whisky
- crushed ice
- 40 ml (1⅓ fl oz) ginger ale

58 RED
hook

—

2–3 ice cubes

+

3 drops
Angostura®
bitters

+

60 ml (2 fl oz) rye
whisky

+

30 ml (1 fl oz) red
vermouth

+

50 ml (1⅔ fl oz)
maraschino
liqueur

→

Stir

Strain into glass

+

1 brandied cherry

MAKES 1 GLASS
PREPARATION: 5 MINUTES

- 2–3 ice cubes
- 3 drops Angostura® bitters
- 60 ml (2 fl oz) rye whisky
- 30 ml (1 fl oz) red vermouth
- 50 ml (1⅔ fl oz) maraschino liqueur
- 1 brandied cherry

59 BERRY *mechanic*
—

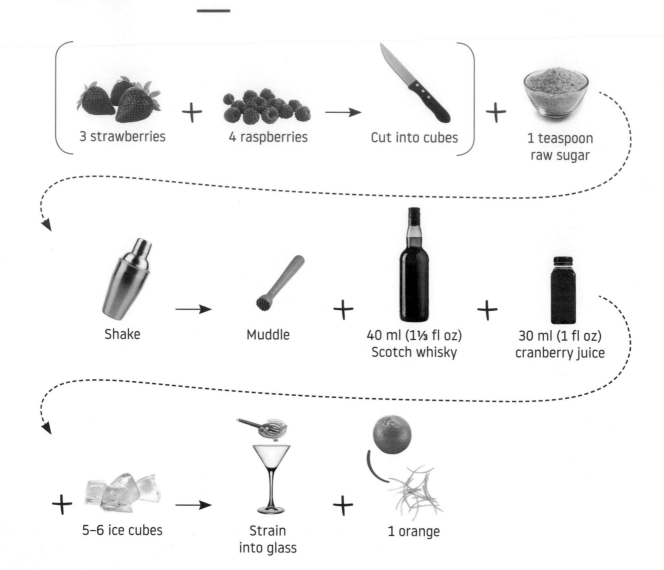

3 strawberries + 4 raspberries → Cut into cubes + 1 teaspoon raw sugar

Shake → Muddle + 40 ml (1⅓ fl oz) Scotch whisky + 30 ml (1 fl oz) cranberry juice

+ 5–6 ice cubes → Strain into glass + 1 orange

MAKES 1 GLASS
PREPARATION: 5 MINUTES

• 3 strawberries
• 4 raspberries
• 1 teaspoon raw sugar
• 40 ml (1⅓ fl oz) Scotch whisky
• 30 ml (1 fl oz) cranberry juice
• 5–6 ice cubes
• 1 orange, lightly squeezed and
  zested

60 SANTA'S LITTLE HELPER
punch

1.8 l (61 fl oz)
rye whisky

+

900 ml (30½ fl
oz) red vermouth

+

1.35 l (45½ fl oz)
sweet apple cider

+

450 ml (15 fl oz)
cane sugar syrup

+

10 dashes
Angostura®
bitters

+

10 cinnamon
sticks

+

6 cloves

→

Or in a large bowl

→

Stir

+

20–25 ice cubes

+

1 orange

+

1 lemon

MAKES 4.5 LITRES (152 FL OZ)
PREPARATION: 10 MINUTES

- 1.8 (61 fl oz) rye whisky
- 900 (30½ fl oz) red vermouth
- 1.35 l (45½ fl oz) sweet apple cider
- 450 ml (15 fl oz) cane sugar syrup
- 10 dashes Angostura® bitters
- 10 cinnamon sticks
- 6 cloves
- 20–25 ice cubes
- 1 orange, sliced
- 1 lemon, sliced

61

CHAMPAGNE
cocktail

—

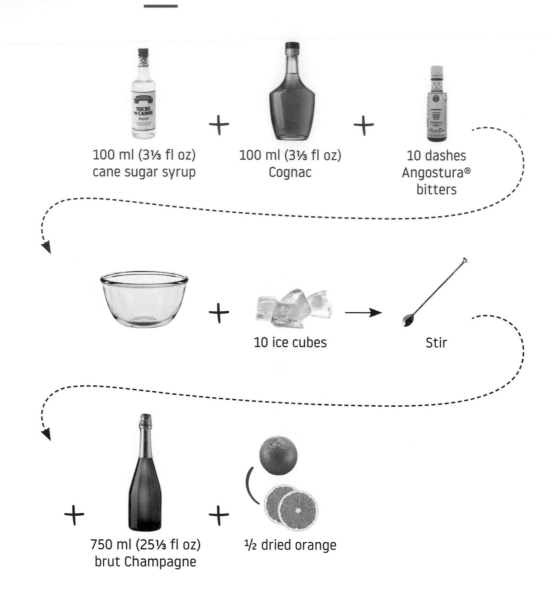

100 ml (3⅓ fl oz)
cane sugar syrup

+

100 ml (3⅓ fl oz)
Cognac

+

10 dashes
Angostura®
bitters

+

10 ice cubes

→ Stir

+

750 ml (25⅓ fl oz)
brut Champagne

+

½ dried orange

MAKES 1 LITRE (34 FL OZ)
PREPARATION: 10 MINUTES

- 100 ml (3⅓ fl oz) cane sugar syrup
- 100 ml (3⅓ fl oz) Cognac
- 10 dashes Angostura® bitters
- 10 ice cubes
- 750 ml (25⅓ fl oz) brut Champagne
- ½ dried orange, sliced

62 KIR
royal

—

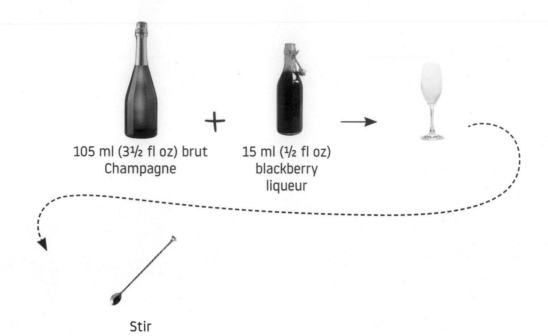

105 ml (3½ fl oz) brut
Champagne

+

15 ml (½ fl oz)
blackberry
liqueur

→

Stir

MAKES 1 GLASS
PREPARATION: 5 MINUTES

_____

- 105 ml (3½ fl oz) brut
  Champagne
- 15 ml (½ fl oz) blackberry
  liqueur

63 MOJITO
royal

———

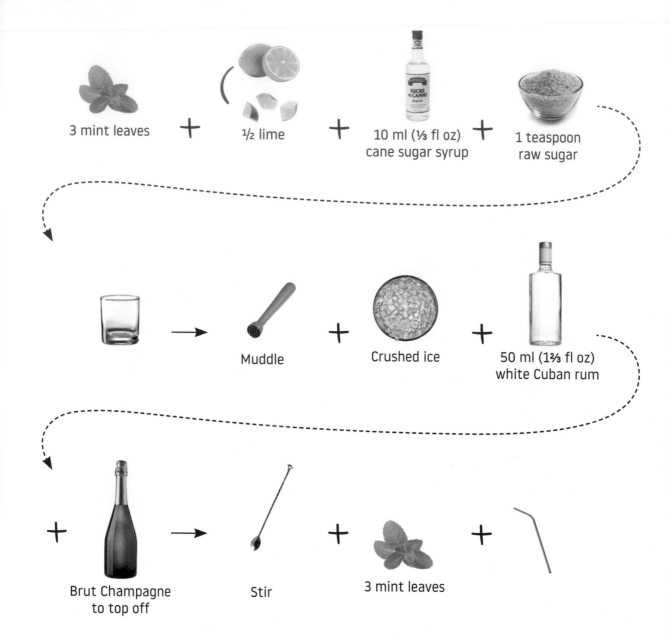

3 mint leaves + ½ lime + 10 ml (⅓ fl oz) cane sugar syrup + 1 teaspoon raw sugar

→ Muddle + Crushed ice + 50 ml (1⅔ fl oz) white Cuban rum

+ Brut Champagne to top off → Stir + 3 mint leaves +

MAKES 1 GLASS
PREPARATION: 5 MINUTES

——————————

- 6 mint leaves
- ½ lime, diced
- 10 ml (⅓ fl oz) cane sugar syrup
- 1 teaspoon raw sugar
- crushed ice
- 50 ml (1⅗ fl oz) white Cuban rum
- brut Champagne to top off

64 RASPBERRY
rossini
—

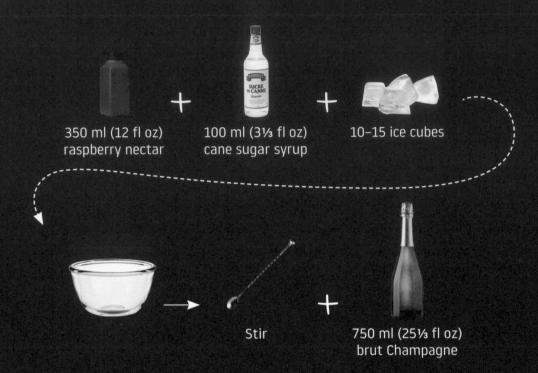

350 ml (12 fl oz)
raspberry nectar

+

100 ml (3⅓ fl oz)
cane sugar syrup

+

10–15 ice cubes

Stir

+

750 ml (25⅓ fl oz)
brut Champagne

MAKES 1.2 LITRES
(40½ FL OZ)
PREPARATION: 5 MINUTES

_____

- 350 ml (12 fl oz) raspberry
  nectar
- 100 ml (3⅓ fl oz) cane sugar
  syrup
- 10–15 ice cubes
- 750 ml (25⅓ fl oz) brut
  Champagne

65 PEACH
bellini
—

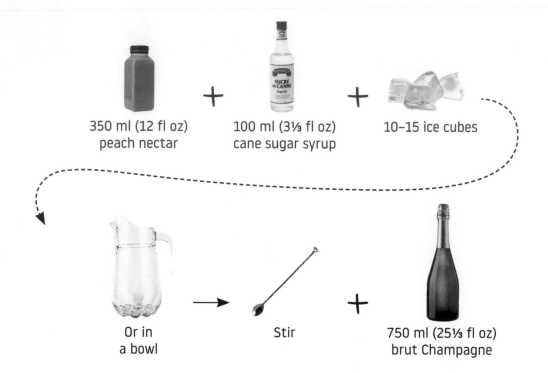

350 ml (12 fl oz)
peach nectar

+

100 ml (3⅓ fl oz)
cane sugar syrup

+

10–15 ice cubes

Or in
a bowl

→ Stir

+

750 ml (25⅓ fl oz)
brut Champagne

MAKES 1.2 LITRES
(40½ FL OZ)
PREPARATION: 5 MINUTES

- 350 ml (12 fl oz) peach nectar
- 100 ml (3⅓ fl oz) cane sugar syrup
- 10–15 ice cubes
- 750 ml (25⅓ fl oz) brut Champagne

66 ORANGE
mimosa
—

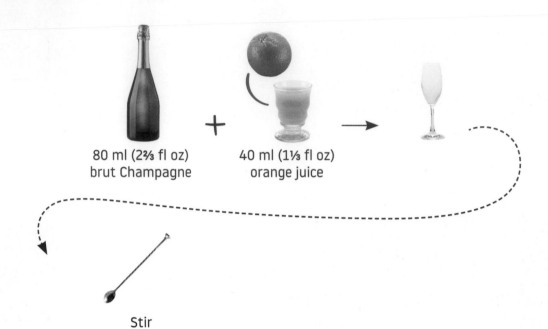

80 ml (2⅔ fl oz)
brut Champagne

+

40 ml (1⅓ fl oz)
orange juice

Stir

MAKES 1 GLASS
PREPARATION: 5 MINUTES

- 80 ml (2⅔ fl oz) brut
  Champagne
- 40 ml (1⅓ fl oz) orange juice

67 CITRUS CHAMPAGNE
punch

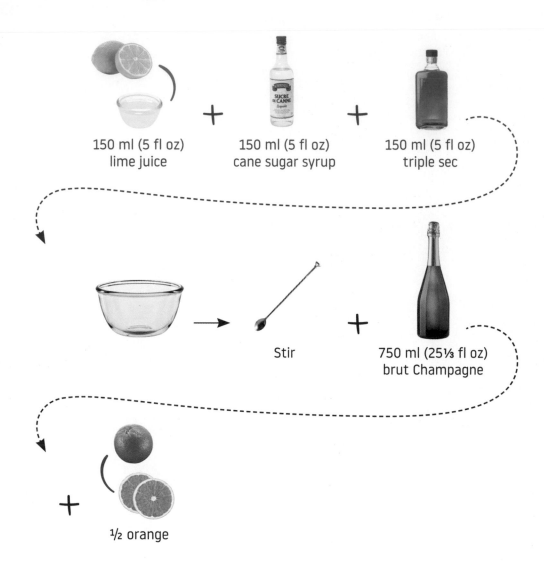

150 ml (5 fl oz)
lime juice

+

150 ml (5 fl oz)
cane sugar syrup

+

150 ml (5 fl oz)
triple sec

Stir

+

750 ml (25⅓ fl oz)
brut Champagne

+

½ orange

MAKES 1.2 LITRES
(40½ FL OZ)
PREPARATION: 10 MINUTES

_____

- 150ml (5 fl oz) lime juice
- 150 ml (5 fl oz) cane sugar syrup
- 150 ml (5 fl oz) triple sec
- 750 ml (25⅓ fl oz) brut Champagne
- ½ orange, sliced

68 REFRESHING
Champagne punch
—

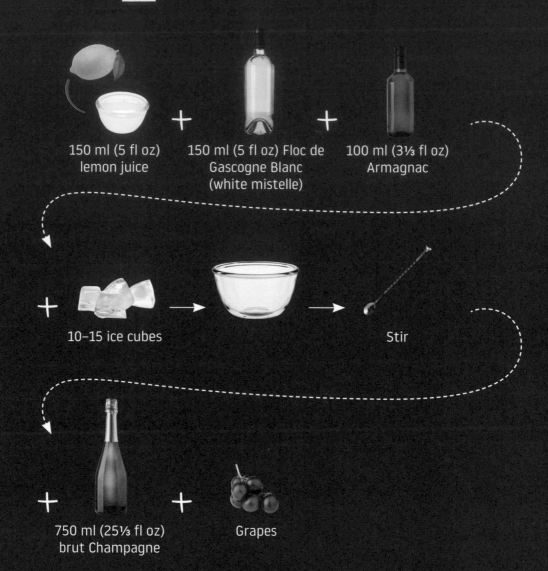

150 ml (5 fl oz)
lemon juice

+

150 ml (5 fl oz) Floc de
Gascogne Blanc
(white mistelle)

+

100 ml (3⅓ fl oz)
Armagnac

+ 10–15 ice cubes → → Stir

+

750 ml (25⅓ fl oz)
brut Champagne

+

Grapes

MAKES 1.15 LITRES (39 FL OZ)
PREPARATION: 5 MINUTES

———————

- 150 ml (5 fl oz) lemon juice
- 150 ml (5 fl oz) Floc de Gascogne Blanc (white mistelle)
- 100 ml (3⅓ fl oz) Armagnac
- 10–15 ice cubes
- 750 ml (25⅓ fl oz) brut Champagne
- grapes

69

SOUPE
Angevine

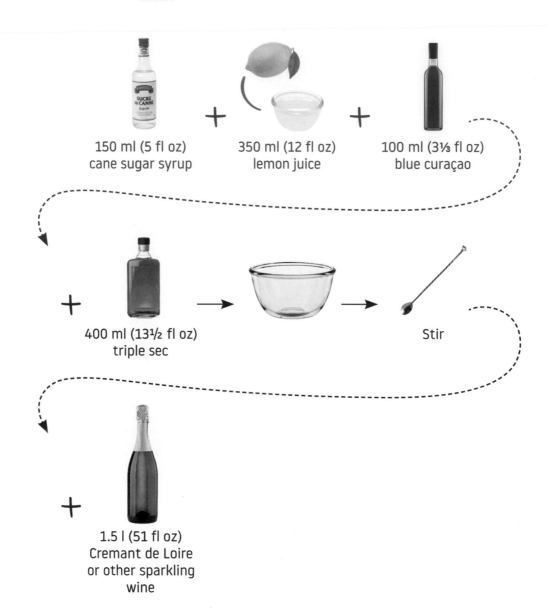

150 ml (5 fl oz)
cane sugar syrup

350 ml (12 fl oz)
lemon juice

100 ml (3⅓ fl oz)
blue curaçao

400 ml (13½ fl oz)
triple sec

Stir

1.5 l (51 fl oz)
Cremant de Loire
or other sparkling
wine

MAKES 2.5 LITRES
(84½ FL OZ)
PREPARATION: 10 MINUTES

————————

- 150 ml (3⅛ fl oz) cane sugar
  syrup
- 350 ml (12 fl oz) lemon juice
- 100 ml (3⅛ fl oz) blue curaçao
- 400 ml (13½ fl oz) triple sec
- 1.5 l (51 fl oz) Cremant de Loire
  or other sparkling wine

70 THE KING
with pommeau
—

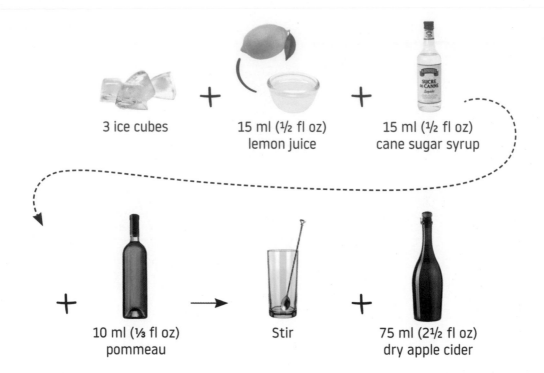

3 ice cubes

+

15 ml (½ fl oz)
lemon juice

+

15 ml (½ fl oz)
cane sugar syrup

+

10 ml (⅓ fl oz)
pommeau

→

Stir

+

75 ml (2½ fl oz)
dry apple cider

- 3 ice cubes
- 15 ml (½ fl oz) lemon juice
- 15 ml (½ fl oz) cane sugar syrup
- 10 ml (⅓ fl oz) pommeau
- 75 ml (2½ fl oz) dry apple cider

71 REVIVER
wheat beer and ginger
—

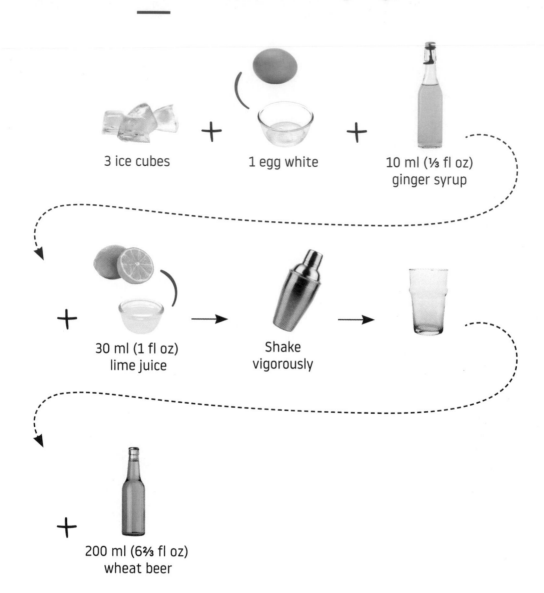

3 ice cubes + 1 egg white + 10 ml (⅓ fl oz) ginger syrup

+ 30 ml (1 fl oz) lime juice → Shake vigorously →

+ 200 ml (6⅔ fl oz) wheat beer

MAKES 1 GLASS
PREPARATION: 5 MINUTES

_____

- 3 ice cubes
- 1 egg white
- 10 ml (⅓ fl oz) ginger syrup
- 30 ml (1 fl oz) lime juice
- 200 ml (6⅔ fl oz) wheat beer

72 ROCK
stout and red wine
—

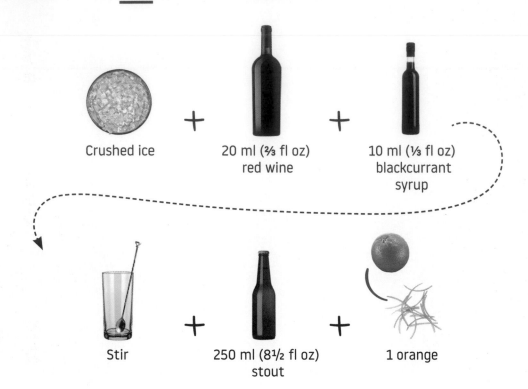

Crushed ice

+

20 ml (⅔ fl oz)
red wine

+

10 ml (⅓ fl oz)
blackcurrant
syrup

Stir

+

250 ml (8½ fl oz)
stout

+

1 orange

MAKES 1 GLASS
PREPARATION: 5 MINUTES

_____

- crushed ice
- 20 ml (⅔ fl oz) red wine
- 10 ml (⅓ fl oz) blackcurrant
  syrup
- 250 ml (8½ fl oz) stout
- 1 orange, lightly squeezed and
  zested

73 LADY *killer*

—

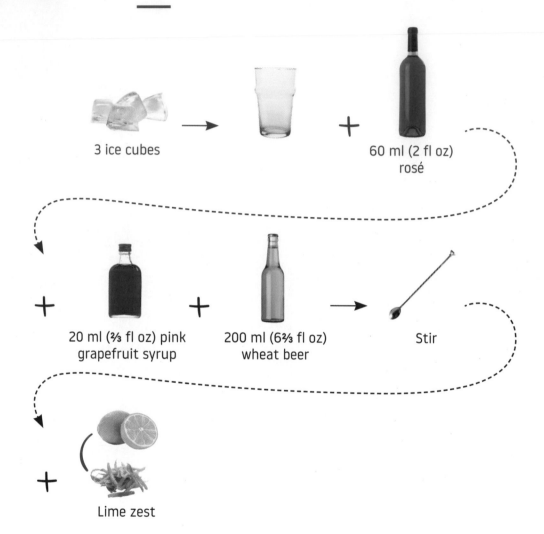

3 ice cubes

+ 60 ml (2 fl oz)
rosé

+ 20 ml (⅔ fl oz) pink
grapefruit syrup

+ 200 ml (6⅔ fl oz)
wheat beer

Stir

+ Lime zest

MAKES 1 GLASS
PREPARATION: 5 MINUTES

- 3 ice cubes
- 60 ml (2 fl oz) rosé
- 20 ml (⅔ fl oz) pink grapefruit syrup
- 200 ml (6⅔ fl oz) wheat beer
- lime zest

74 WHITE
sangria
—

4 limes + 2 grapefruit + 3 mandarins

+ 6 raspberries + 200 g (7 oz) sugar + 300 ml (10 fl oz) sherry

24 HOURS Macerate in the refrigerator + Crushed ice

+ 1.5 l (51 fl oz) white wine → Stir

MAKES 1.8 LITRES (61 FL OZ)
PREPARATION: 10 MINUTES
MACERATION: 24 HOURS

———————————

- 4 limes, sliced
- 2 grapefruit, cut into quarter slices
- 3 mandarins, segmented
- 6 raspberries
- 200 g (7 oz) sugar
- 300 ml (10 fl oz) sherry
- crushed ice
- 1.5 l (51 fl oz) white wine

75 ITALIAN
dream
—

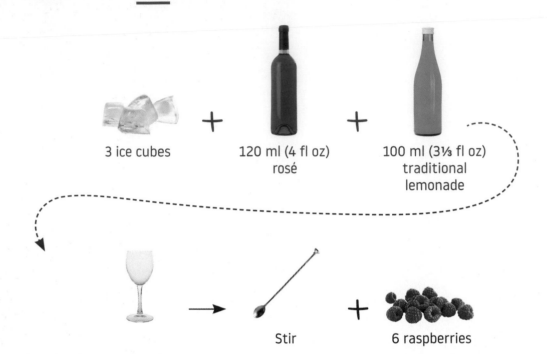

3 ice cubes + 120 ml (4 fl oz) rosé + 100 ml (3⅓ fl oz) traditional lemonade

→ Stir + 6 raspberries

MAKES 1 GLASS
PREPARATION: 5 MINUTES

- 3 ice cubes
- 120 ml (4 fl oz) rosé
- 100 ml (3⅓ fl oz) traditional lemonade
- 6 raspberries

76 ROSY
spritz

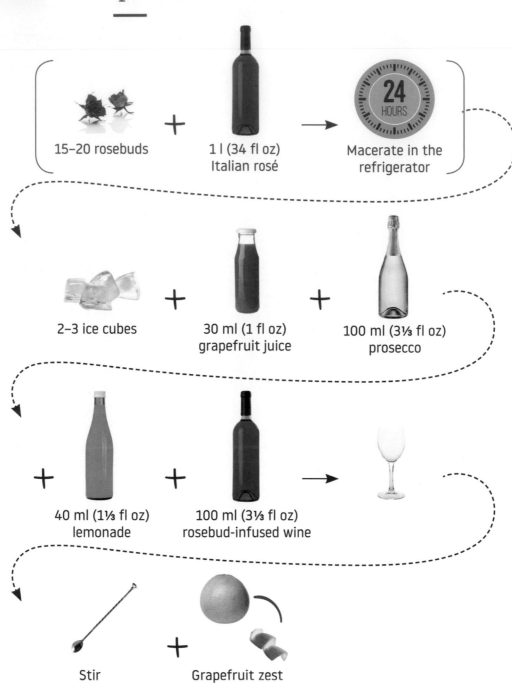

15–20 rosebuds + 1 l (34 fl oz) Italian rosé → 24 HOURS Macerate in the refrigerator

2–3 ice cubes + 30 ml (1 fl oz) grapefruit juice + 100 ml (3⅓ fl oz) prosecco

+ 40 ml (1⅓ fl oz) lemonade + 100 ml (3⅓ fl oz) rosebud-infused wine →

Stir + Grapefruit zest

MAKES 1 GLASS
PREPARATION: 5 MINUTES
MACERATION: 24 HOURS

———————

• 15–20 rosebuds
• 100 ml (3⅓ fl oz) Italian rosé
• 2–3 ice cubes
• 30 ml (1 fl oz) grapefruit juice
• 100 ml (3⅓ fl oz) prosecco
• 40 ml (3⅓ fl oz) lemonade
• grapefruit zest

77 RED
sangria

—

750 ml
(25⅓ fl oz) Rioja

+

60 ml (2 fl oz)
cognac

+

60 ml (2 fl oz)
triple sec

+

60 ml (2 fl oz)
orange juice

+

6 sugar cubes

+

1 cinnamon stick

→ → Stir

4 HOURS

Macerate
in the refrigerator

+

18 ice cubes

+

250 ml (8½ fl oz)
sparkling water

+

10 lime slices

+

10 lesliceslices

+

10 orange
slices

→ Stir

MAKES 1.2 LITRES
(40½ FL OZ)
PREPARATION: 10 MINUTES
MACERATION: 4 HOURS

———————

- 750 ml (25⅓ fl oz) Rioja
- 60 ml (2 fl oz) cognac
- 60 ml (2 fl oz) triple sec
- 60 ml (2 fl oz) orange juice
- 6 sugar cubes
- 1 cinnamon stick
- 18 ice cubes
- 250 ml (8½ fl oz) sparkling water
- 10 lime slices
- 10 lemon slices
- 10 orange slices

78 SPICED
mulled wine
—

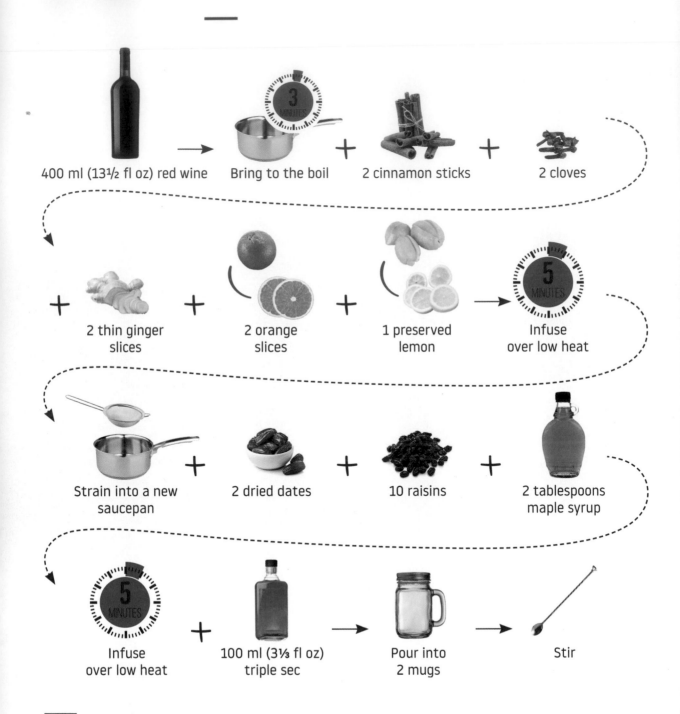

400 ml (13½ fl oz) red wine → Bring to the boil **3 MINUTES** + 2 cinnamon sticks + 2 cloves

+ 2 thin ginger slices + 2 orange slices + 1 preserved lemon → Infuse over low heat **5 MINUTES**

Strain into a new saucepan + 2 dried dates + 10 raisins + 2 tablespoons maple syrup

Infuse over low heat **5 MINUTES** + 100 ml (3⅓ fl oz) triple sec → Pour into 2 mugs → Stir

MAKES 2 GLASSES
PREPARATION: 5 MINUTES
COOKING: 13 MINUTES

———————————

- 400 ml (13½ fl oz) red wine
- 2 cinnamon sticks
- 2 cloves
- 2 thin ginger slices
- 2 orange slices
- 1 preserved lemon
- 2 dried dates
- 10 raisins
- 2 tablespoons maple syrup
- 100 ml (3⅓ fl oz) triple sec

79 DOLCE
spritz
—

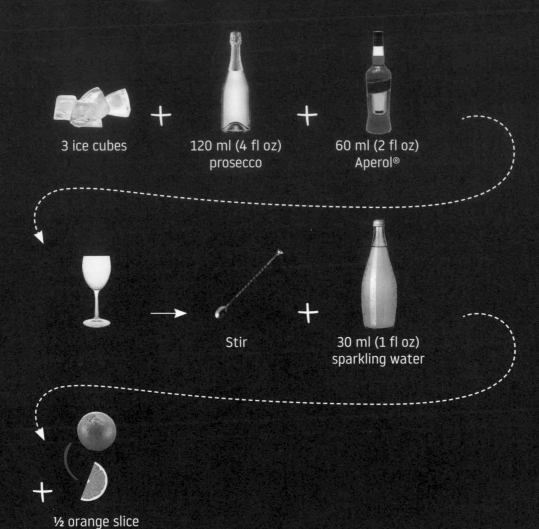

3 ice cubes + 120 ml (4 fl oz) prosecco + 60 ml (2 fl oz) Aperol®

Stir + 30 ml (1 fl oz) sparkling water

+ ½ orange slice

MAKES 1 GLASS
PREPARATION: 5 MINUTES

- 3 ice cubes
- 120 ml (4 fl oz) prosecco
- 60 ml (2 fl oz) Aperol®
- 30 ml (1 fl oz) sparkling water
- ½ orange slice

80 GREEN
fairy
—

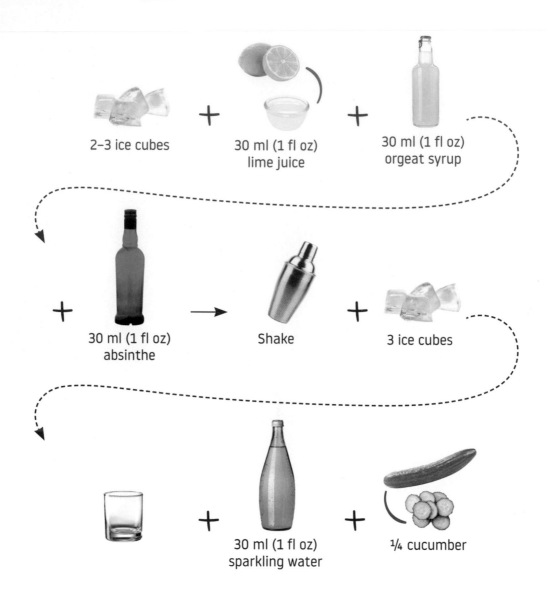

2–3 ice cubes

\+

30 ml (1 fl oz)
lime juice

\+

30 ml (1 fl oz)
orgeat syrup

\+

30 ml (1 fl oz)
absinthe

→ Shake

\+

3 ice cubes

\+

30 ml (1 fl oz)
sparkling water

\+

¼ cucumber

MAKES 1 GLASS
PREPARATION: 5 MINUTES

- 6 ice cubes
- 30 ml (1 fl oz) lime juice
- 30 ml (1 fl oz) orgeat syrup
- 30 ml (1 fl oz) absinthe
- 30 ml (1 fl oz) sparkling water
- ¼ cucumber, sliced

81 BITTER
spritz
—

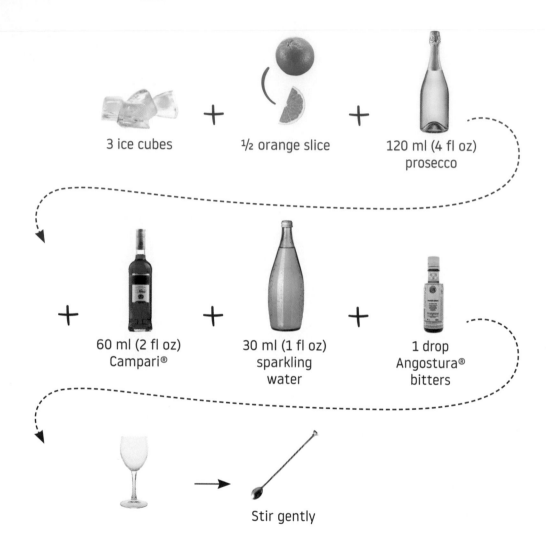

3 ice cubes   +   ½ orange slice   +   120 ml (4 fl oz) prosecco

+   60 ml (2 fl oz) Campari®   +   30 ml (1 fl oz) sparkling water   +   1 drop Angostura® bitters

→   Stir gently

MAKES 1 GLASS
PREPARATION: 5 MINUTES

- 3 ice cubes
- ½ orange slice
- 120 ml (4 fl oz) prosecco
- 60 ml (2 fl oz) Campari®
- 30 ml (1 fl oz) sparkling water
- 1 drop Angostura® bitters

82 FROZEN LADY
spritz

—

30 ml (1 fl oz)
elderflower
liqueur

+

60 ml (2 fl oz)
rosé

+

120 ml (4 fl oz)
prosecco

+ 4 strawberries + Crushed ice → Blend to make a granita

+ 1 strawberry + ½ pink grapefruit slice

MAKES 1 GLASS
PREPARATION: 5 MINUTES

_____

- 30 ml (1 fl oz) elderflower liqueur
- 60 ml (2 fl oz) rosé
- 120 ml (4 fl oz) prosecco
- 5 strawberries
- crushed ice
- ½ pink grapefruit slice

83

PINEAPPLE
cognac surprise

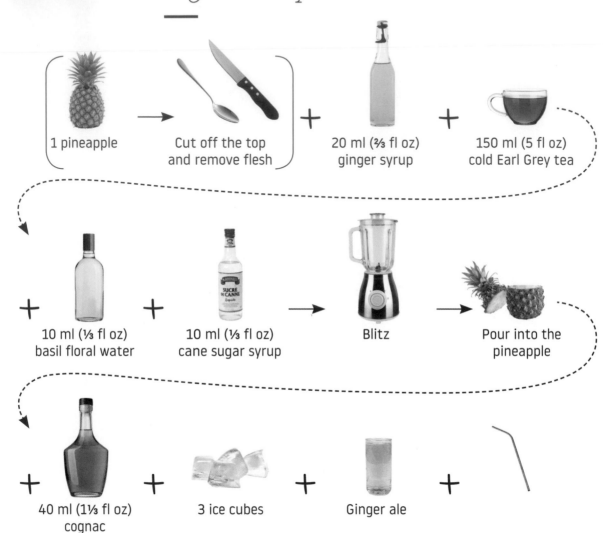

1 pineapple → Cut off the top and remove flesh

+ 20 ml (⅔ fl oz) ginger syrup

+ 150 ml (5 fl oz) cold Earl Grey tea

+ 10 ml (⅓ fl oz) basil floral water

+ 10 ml (⅓ fl oz) cane sugar syrup

→ Blitz

→ Pour into the pineapple

+ 40 ml (1⅓ fl oz) cognac

+ 3 ice cubes

+ Ginger ale

+

MAKES 1 GLASS
PREPARATION: 5 MINUTES

- 1 pineapple, flesh removed
- 20 ml (⅔ fl oz) ginger syrup
- 150 ml (5 fl oz) cold Earl Grey tea
- 10 ml (⅓ fl oz) basil floral water
- 10 ml (⅓ fl oz) cane sugar syrup
- 40 ml (1⅓ fl oz) cognac
- 3 ice cubes
- ginger ale

84 COGNAC
in China
—

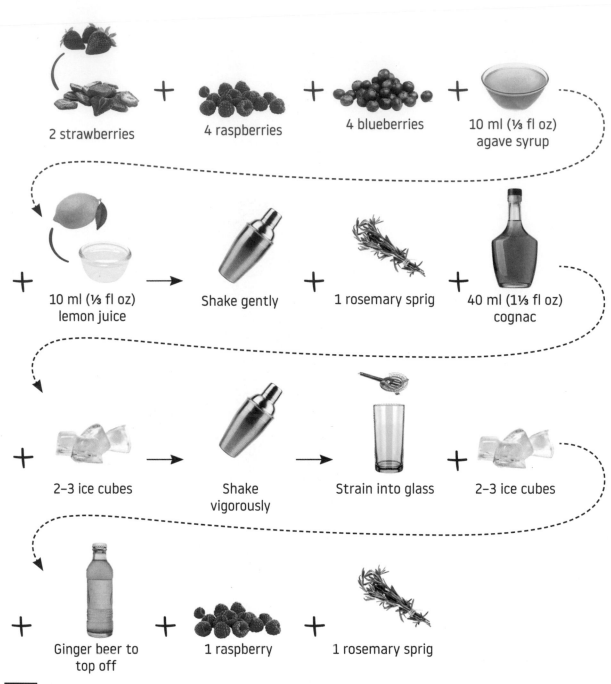

2 strawberries + 4 raspberries + 4 blueberries + 10 ml (⅓ fl oz) agave syrup

+ 10 ml (⅓ fl oz) lemon juice → Shake gently + 1 rosemary sprig + 40 ml (1⅓ fl oz) cognac

+ 2–3 ice cubes → Shake vigorously → Strain into glass + 2–3 ice cubes

+ Ginger beer to top off + 1 raspberry + 1 rosemary sprig

MAKES 1 GLASS
PREPARATION: 5 MINUTES

_____

- 2 strawberries
- 5 raspberries
- 4 blueberries
- 10 ml (⅓ fl oz) agave syrup
- 10 ml (⅓ fl oz) lemon juice
- 2 rosemary sprigs
- 40 ml (1⅓ fl oz) cognac
- 6 ice cubes
- ginger beer

85

SMOKED
gourmet

—

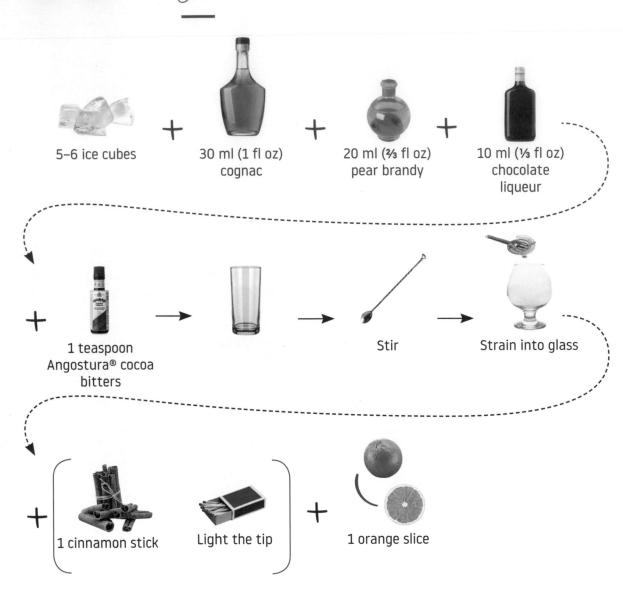

5–6 ice cubes + 30 ml (1 fl oz) cognac + 20 ml (⅔ fl oz) pear brandy + 10 ml (⅓ fl oz) chocolate liqueur

+ 1 teaspoon Angostura® cocoa bitters → → Stir → Strain into glass

+ [1 cinnamon stick   Light the tip] + 1 orange slice

MAKES 1 GLASS
PREPARATION: 5 MINUTES

———————

- 5–6 ice cubes
- 30 ml (1 fl oz) cognac
- 20 ml (⅔ fl oz) pear brandy
- 10 ml (⅓ fl oz) chocolate
  liqueur
- 1 teaspoon Angostura® cocoa
  bitters
- 1 cinnamon stick
- 1 orange slice

86 MY MEDICINE
with bourbon
—

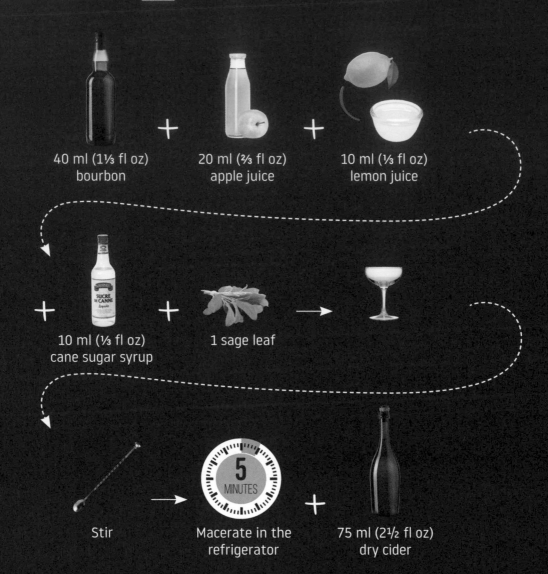

40 ml (1⅓ fl oz)
bourbon

+

20 ml (⅔ fl oz)
apple juice

+

10 ml (⅓ fl oz)
lemon juice

+

10 ml (⅓ fl oz)
cane sugar syrup

+

1 sage leaf

→

Stir

→

5
MINUTES

Macerate in the
refrigerator

+

75 ml (2½ fl oz)
dry cider

MAKES 1 GLASS
PREPARATION: 5 MINUTES
MACERATION: 5 MINUTES

———————

- 40 ml (1⅓ fl oz) bourbon
- 20 ml (⅔ fl oz) apple juice
- 10 ml (⅓ fl oz) lemon juice
- 10 ml (⅓ fl oz) cane sugar syrup
- 1 sage leaf
- 75 ml (2½ fl oz) dry cider

87 SUZIE
spritz

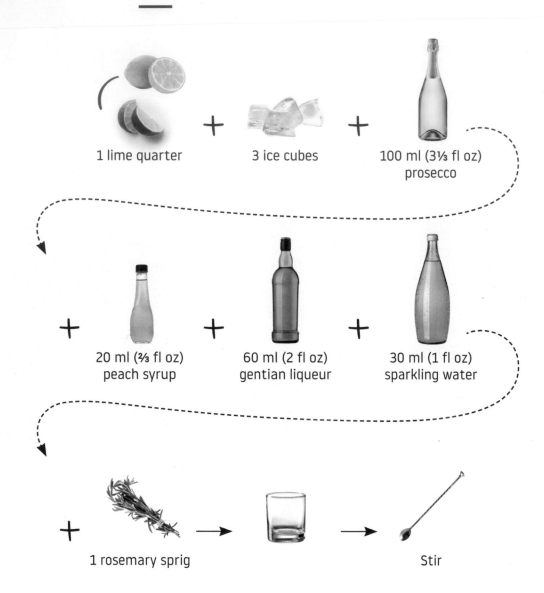

1 lime quarter + 3 ice cubes + 100 ml (3⅓ fl oz) prosecco

+ 20 ml (⅔ fl oz) peach syrup + 60 ml (2 fl oz) gentian liqueur + 30 ml (1 fl oz) sparkling water

+ 1 rosemary sprig → Stir

MAKES 1 GLASS
PREPARATION: 5 MINUTES

- 1 lime quarter
- 3 ice cubes
- 100 ml (3⅓ fl oz) prosecco
- 20 ml (⅔ fl oz) peach syrup
- 60 ml (2 fl oz) gentian liqueur
  (such as Suze®)
- 30 ml (1 fl oz) sparkling water
- 1 rosemary sprig

88

SUZE®
of the mountains

—

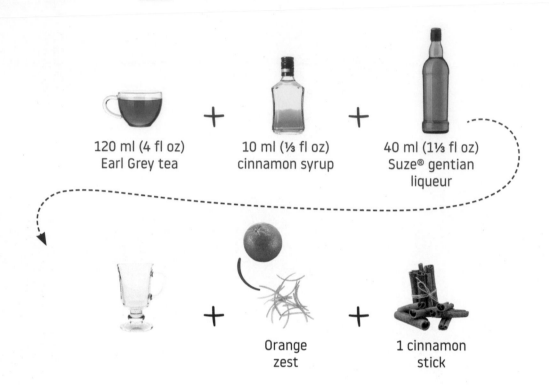

120 ml (4 fl oz)
Earl Grey tea

+

10 ml (⅓ fl oz)
cinnamon syrup

+

40 ml (1⅓ fl oz)
Suze® gentian
liqueur

Orange
zest

+

1 cinnamon
stick

MAKES 1 GLASS
PREPARATION: 5 MINUTES

———————

• 120 ml (4 fl oz) Earl Grey tea
• 10 ml (⅓ fl oz) cinnamon syrup
• 40 ml (1⅓ fl oz) gentian liqueur
  (such as Suze®)
• orange zest
• 1 cinnamon stick

89

PIMM'S®
cocktail

—

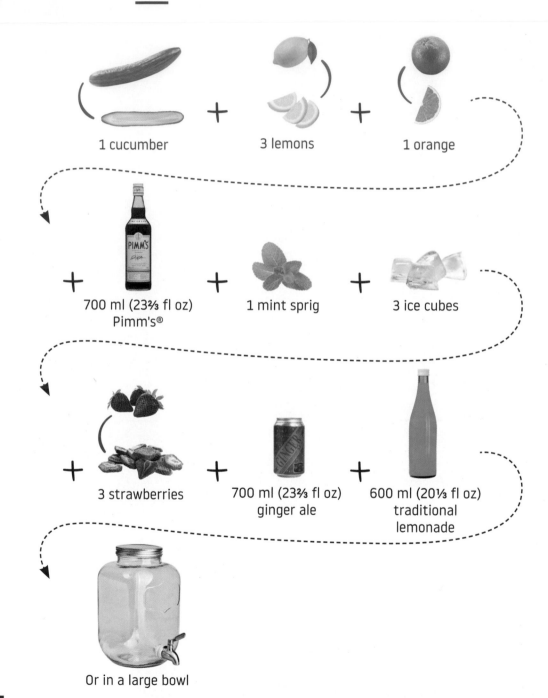

1 cucumber   +   3 lemons   +   1 orange

+   700 ml (23⅔ fl oz) Pimm's®   +   1 mint sprig   +   3 ice cubes

+   3 strawberries   +   700 ml (23⅔ fl oz) ginger ale   +   600 ml (20⅓ fl oz) traditional lemonade

Or in a large bowl

MAKES 2 LITRES (68 FL OZ)
PREPARATION: 10 MINUTES

_____

- 1 cucumber, cut into long strips
- 3 lemons, sliced
- 1 orange, sliced
- 700 ml (23⅔ fl oz) Pimm's®
- 1 mint sprig
- 3 ice cubes
- 3 strawberries
- 700 ml (23⅔ fl oz) ginger ale
- 600 ml (20⅓ fl oz) traditional lemonade

90 CITRUS, STRAWBERRY
and triple sec float

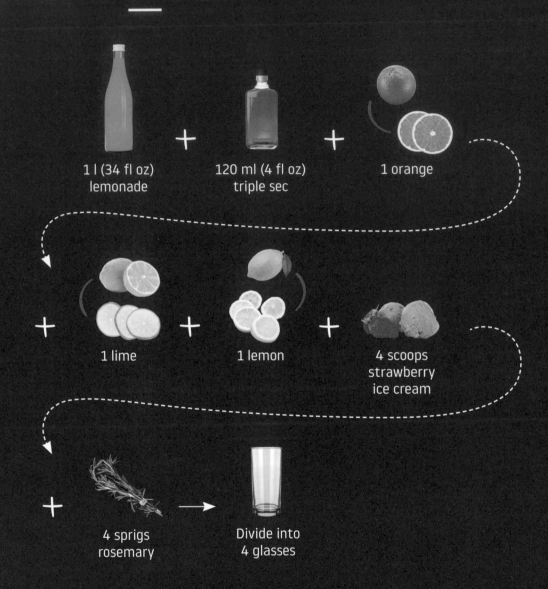

1 l (34 fl oz) lemonade

+

120 ml (4 fl oz) triple sec

+

1 orange

+

1 lime

+

1 lemon

+

4 scoops strawberry ice cream

+

4 sprigs rosemary

→ Divide into 4 glasses

- 1 l (34 fl oz) lemonade
- 120 ml (4 fl oz) triple sec
- 1 orange, sliced
- 1 lime, sliced
- 1 lemon, sliced
- 4 scoops strawberry ice cream
- 4 sprigs rosemary

91

SALTY OLD
bastard
—

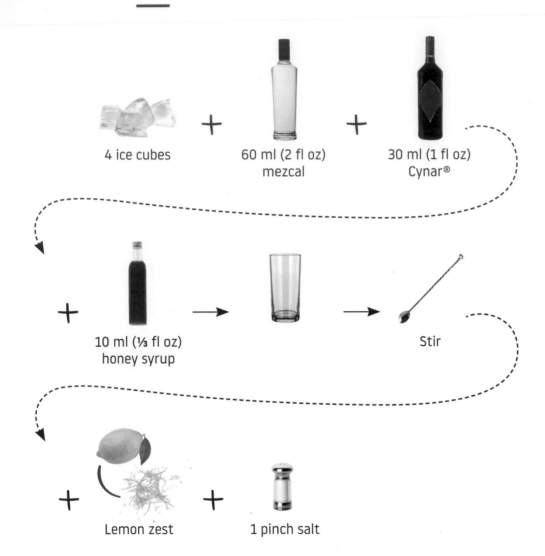

4 ice cubes + 60 ml (2 fl oz) mezcal + 30 ml (1 fl oz) Cynar®

+ 10 ml (⅓ fl oz) honey syrup → [glass] → Stir

+ Lemon zest + 1 pinch salt

MAKES 1 GLASS
PREPARATION: 5 MINUTES

- 4 ice cubes
- 60 ml (2 fl oz) mezcal
- 30 ml (1 fl oz) Cynar®
- 10 ml (⅓ fl oz) honey syrup
- lemon zest
- 1 pinch salt

92 VIRGIN
mojito
—

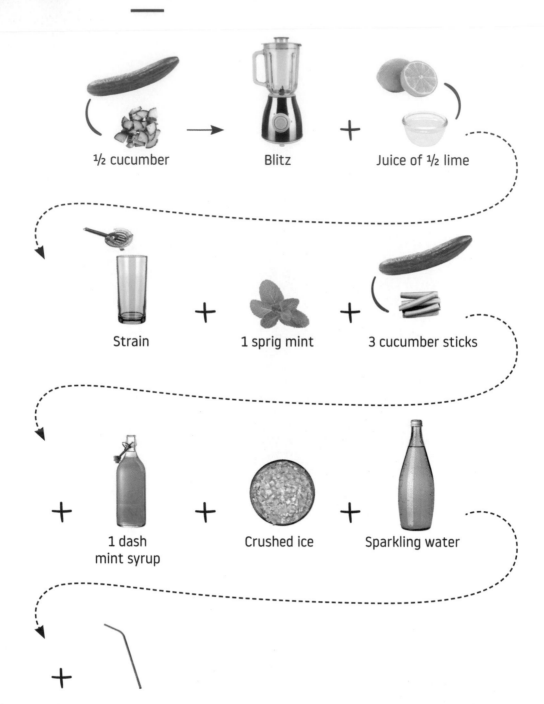

½ cucumber → Blitz + Juice of ½ lime

Strain + 1 sprig mint + 3 cucumber sticks

+ 1 dash mint syrup + Crushed ice + Sparkling water

+

MAKES 1 GLASS
PREPARATION: 5 MINUTES

• ½ cucumber, chopped + 3 sticks
• ½ lime, juiced
• 1 sprig mint
• 1 dash mint syrup
• crushed ice
• sparkling water

93

POMELO
mojito

—

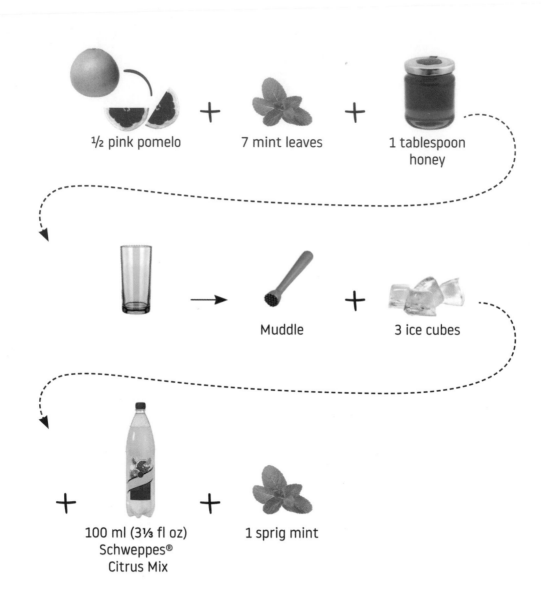

½ pink pomelo + 7 mint leaves + 1 tablespoon honey

→ Muddle + 3 ice cubes

+ 100 ml (3⅓ fl oz) Schweppes® Citrus Mix + 1 sprig mint

MAKES 1 GLASS
PREPARATION: 5 MINUTES

• ½ pink pomelo, sliced
• 7 mint leaves + 1 sprig
• 1 tablespoon honey
• 3 ice cubes
• 100 ml (3⅓ fl oz) Schweppes®
  Citrus Mix

94

HEAVY-DUTY
cranberry, hibiscus and pepper

—

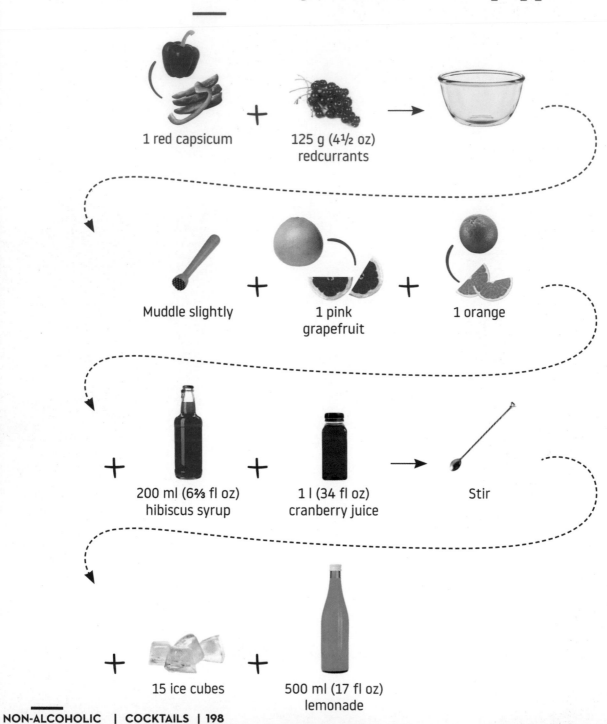

1 red capsicum + 125 g (4½ oz) redcurrants →

Muddle slightly + 1 pink grapefruit + 1 orange

+ 200 ml (6⅔ fl oz) hibiscus syrup + 1 l (34 fl oz) cranberry juice → Stir

+ 15 ice cubes + 500 ml (17 fl oz) lemonade

MAKES 1.7 LITRES (60 FL OZ)
PREPARATION: 10 MINUTES

- 1 red capsicum, cut into strips
- 125 g (4½ oz) redcurrants
- 1 pink grapefruit, cut into half slices
- 1 orange, cut into half slices
- 200 ml (6⅔ fl oz) hibiscus syrup
- 1 l (34 fl oz) cranberry juice
- 15 ice cubes
- 500 ml (17 fl oz) lemonade

95 GINGER
lemonade

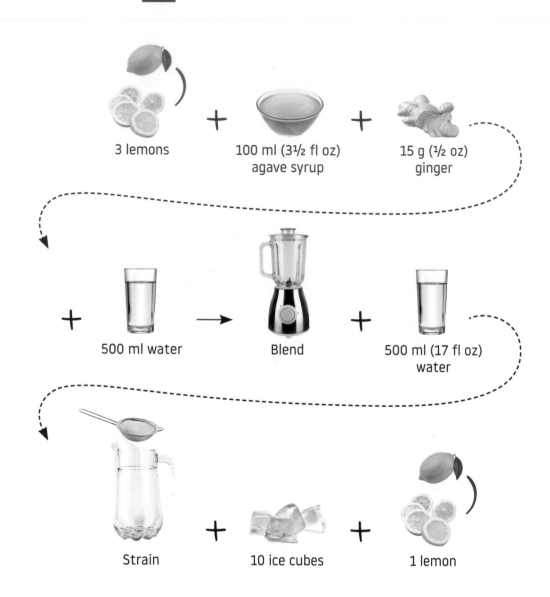

3 lemons + 100 ml (3½ fl oz) agave syrup + 15 g (½ oz) ginger

+ 500 ml water → Blend + 500 ml (17 fl oz) water

Strain + 10 ice cubes + 1 lemon

MAKES 1.1 LITRES (37 FL OZ)
PREPARATION: 10 MINUTES

- 4 lemons, sliced
- 100 ml (3½ fl oz) agave syrup
- 15 g (½ oz) ginger
- 1 l (34 fl oz) water
- 10 ice cubes

96 WELCOME
to paradise

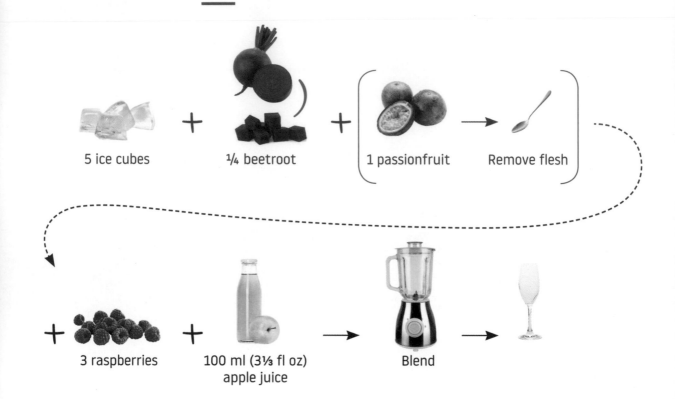

5 ice cubes + ¼ beetroot + 1 passionfruit → Remove flesh

+ 3 raspberries + 100 ml (3⅓ fl oz) apple juice → Blend →

MAKES 1 GLASS
PREPARATION: 5 MINUTES

—————

- 5 ice cubes
- ¼ beetroot, diced
- 1 passionfruit, flesh removed
- 3 raspberries
- 100 ml (3⅓ fl oz) apple juice

97 PANAME
mango, pineapple and passionfruit

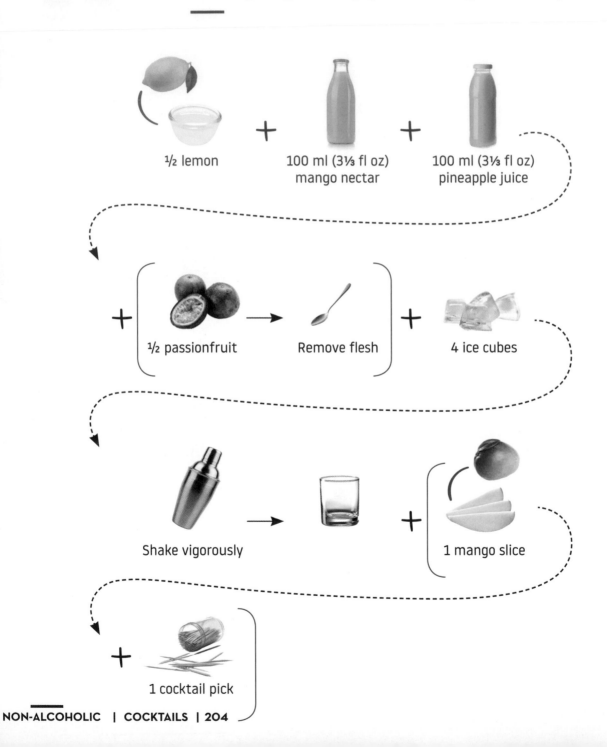

½ lemon

+

100 ml (3⅓ fl oz)
mango nectar

+

100 ml (3⅓ fl oz)
pineapple juice

+

½ passionfruit → Remove flesh

+

4 ice cubes

Shake vigorously →

+

1 mango slice

+

1 cocktail pick

MAKES 1 GLASS
PREPARATION: 5 MINUTES

- ½ lemon, juiced
- 100 ml (3⅓ fl oz) mango nectar
- 100 ml (3⅓ fl oz) pineapple juice
- ½ passionfruit, flesh removed
- 4 ice cubes
- 1 mango slice

98 ITALIAN
detox
—

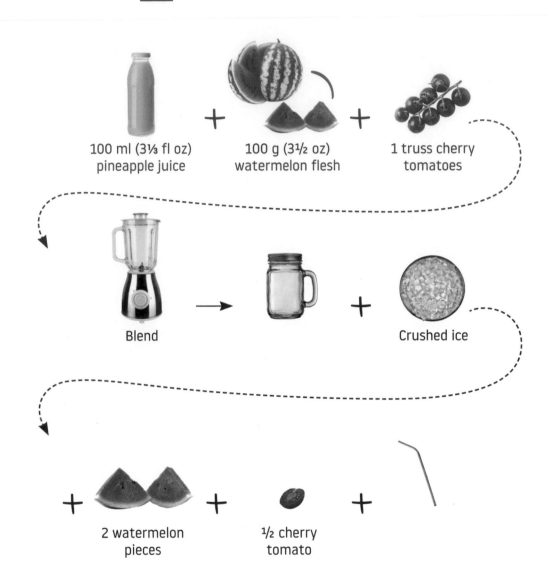

100 ml (3⅓ fl oz)
pineapple juice

+

100 g (3½ oz)
watermelon flesh

+

1 truss cherry
tomatoes

Blend

Crushed ice

+

2 watermelon
pieces

+

½ cherry
tomato

+

MAKES 1 GLASS
PREPARATION: 5 MINUTES

———————

• 100 ml (3⅓ fl oz) pineapple juice
• 100 g (3½ oz) watermelon flesh, diced + 2 pieces
• 1 truss cherry tomatoes + ½ cherry tomato
• crushed ice

99

BANANOCOCO
with vanilla ice cream

—

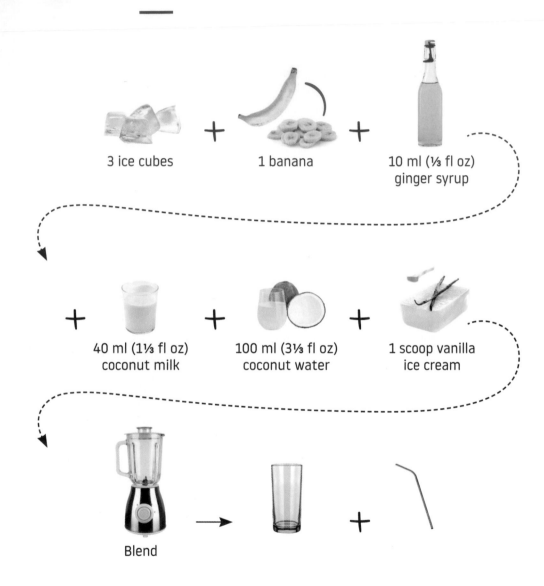

3 ice cubes + 1 banana + 10 ml (⅓ fl oz) ginger syrup

+ 40 ml (1⅓ fl oz) coconut milk + 100 ml (3⅓ fl oz) coconut water + 1 scoop vanilla ice cream

Blend → +

MAKES 1 GLASS
PREPARATION: 5 MINUTES

- 3 ice cubes
- 1 banana, sliced
- 10 ml (⅓ fl oz) ginger syrup
- 40 ml (1⅓ fl oz) coconut milk
- 100 ml (3⅓ fl oz) coconut water
- 1 scoop vanilla ice cream

100 SUMMER
kiss

—

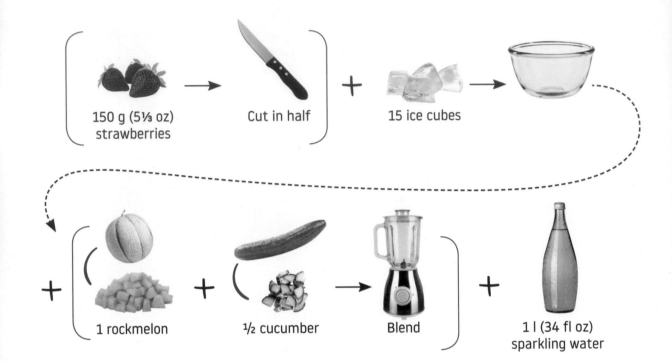

150 g (5⅓ oz) strawberries → Cut in half + 15 ice cubes →

+ 1 rockmelon + ½ cucumber → Blend + 1 l (34 fl oz) sparkling water

MAKES 1.5 LITRES (51 FL OZ)
PREPARATION: 10 MINUTES

———————

- 150 g (5⅓ oz) strawberries,
  halved
- 15 ice cubes
- 1 rockmelon, diced
- ½ cucumber, diced
- 1 l (34 fl oz) sparkling water

101 LUSCIOUS
lemon

—

¼ rockmelon

+

3 sprigs coriander

+

Lime zest

+

5 ice cubes

Blend

+

1 scoop lemon sorbet

+

MAKES 1 GLASS
PREPARATION: 5 MINUTES

———————

- ¼ rockmelon, diced
- 3 sprigs coriander
- lime zest
- 5 ice cubes
- 1 scoop lemon sorbet

102 CRAZY
cucumber

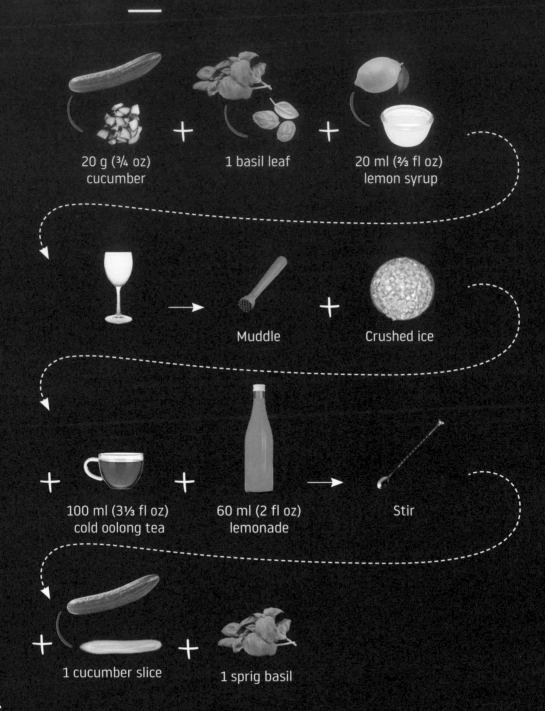

20 g (¾ oz) cucumber

+

1 basil leaf

+

20 ml (⅔ fl oz) lemon syrup

Muddle

+

Crushed ice

+

100 ml (3⅓ fl oz) cold oolong tea

+

60 ml (2 fl oz) lemonade

Stir

+

1 cucumber slice

+

1 sprig basil

MAKES 1 GLASS
PREPARATION: 5 MINUTES

_____

- 20 g (¾ oz) cucumber, diced + 1 lengthways slice
- 1 basil leaf + 1 sprig basil
- 20 ml (⅔ fl oz) lemon syrup
- crushed ice
- 100 ml (3⅓ fl oz) cold oolong tea
- 60 ml (2 fl oz) lemonade

103 REFRESH
cucumber, apple and chilli

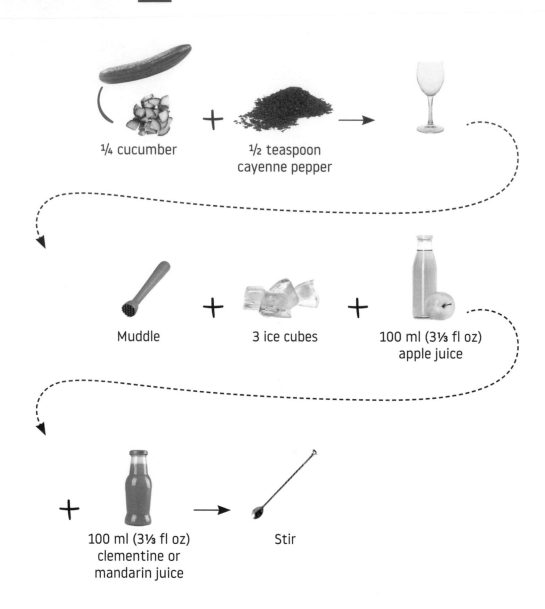

¼ cucumber + ½ teaspoon cayenne pepper →

Muddle + 3 ice cubes + 100 ml (3⅓ fl oz) apple juice

+ 100 ml (3⅓ fl oz) clementine or mandarin juice → Stir

MAKES 1 GLASS
PREPARATION: 5 MINUTES

_____

- ¼ cucumber, diced
- ½ teaspoon cayenne pepper
- 3 ice cubes
- 100 ml (3⅓ fl oz) apple juice
- 100 ml (3⅓ fl oz) clementine or mandarin juice

104 KIWI CUCUMBER *cooler*

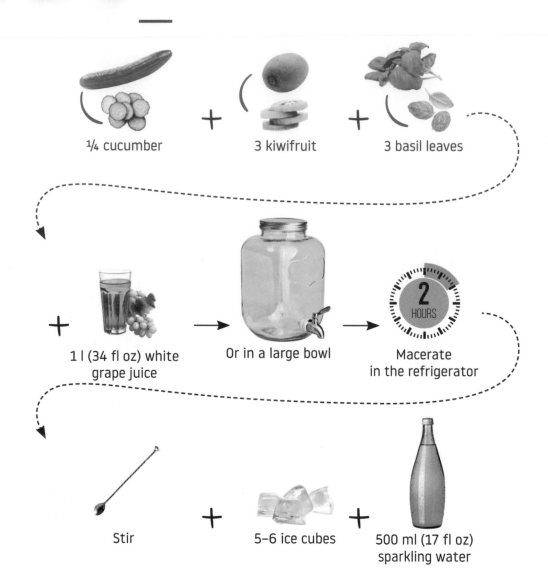

¼ cucumber + 3 kiwifruit + 3 basil leaves

+ 1 l (34 fl oz) white grape juice → Or in a large bowl → Macerate in the refrigerator — **2 HOURS**

Stir + 5–6 ice cubes + 500 ml (17 fl oz) sparkling water

MAKES 1.5 LITRES (51 FL OZ)
PREPARATION: 10 MINUTES
MACERATION: 2 HOURS

- ¼ cucumber, sliced
- 3 kiwifruit, sliced
- 3 basil leaves
- 1 l (34 fl oz) white grape juice
- 5–6 ice cubes
- 500 ml (17 fl oz) sparkling water

105 BUGS *Bunny*

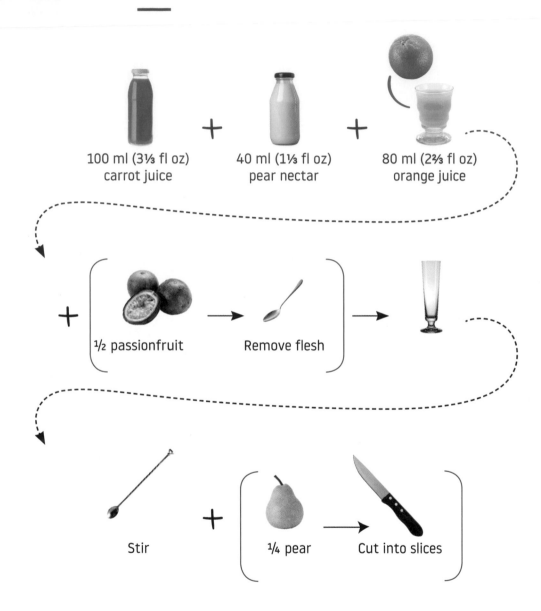

100 ml (3⅓ fl oz)
carrot juice

+

40 ml (1⅓ fl oz)
pear nectar

+

80 ml (2⅔ fl oz)
orange juice

+

½ passionfruit → Remove flesh →

Stir

+

¼ pear → Cut into slices

MAKES 1 GLASS
PREPARATION: 5 MINUTES

- 100 ml (3⅓ fl oz) carrot juice
- 40 ml (1⅓ fl oz) pear nectar
- 80 ml (2⅔ fl oz) orange juice
- ½ passionfruit, flesh removed
- ¼ pear, sliced

106 SUMMER
idea

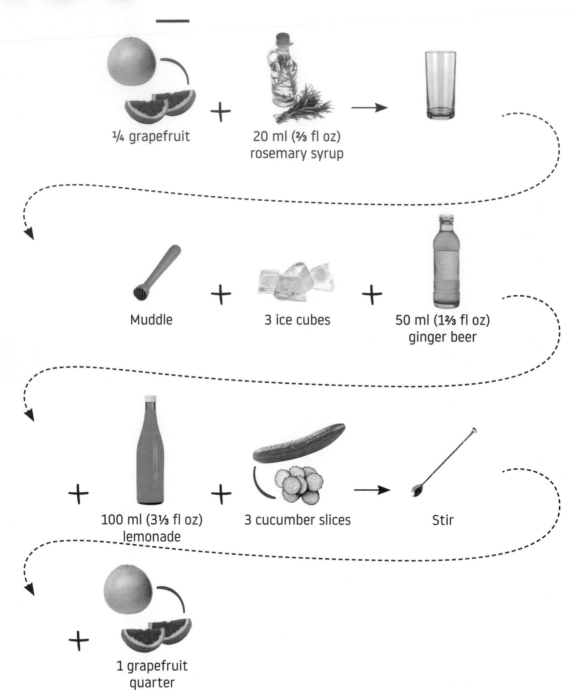

¼ grapefruit

20 ml (⅔ fl oz)
rosemary syrup

Muddle

3 ice cubes

50 ml (1⅔ fl oz)
ginger beer

100 ml (3⅓ fl oz)
lemonade

3 cucumber slices

Stir

1 grapefruit
quarter

MAKES 1 GLASS
PREPARATION: 5 MINUTES

- ¼ grapefruit, cut in half slices
  + 1 grapefruit quarter
- 20 ml (⅔ fl oz) rosemary syrup
- 3 ice cubes
- 50 ml (1⅔ fl oz) ginger beer
- 100 ml (3⅓ fl oz) lemonade
- 3 cucumber slices

107 MAJORELLE'S
garden
—

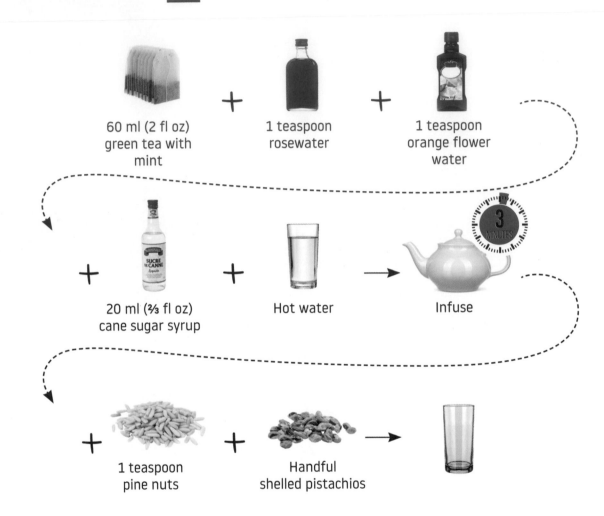

60 ml (2 fl oz)
green tea with
mint

+

1 teaspoon
rosewater

+

1 teaspoon
orange flower
water

+

20 ml (⅔ fl oz)
cane sugar syrup

+

Hot water

→

Infuse

3 MINUTES

+

1 teaspoon
pine nuts

+

Handful
shelled pistachios

→

MAKES 1 GLASS
PREPARATION: 3 MINUTES

———————

- 60 ml (2 fl oz) green tea with mint
- 1 teaspoon rosewater
- 1 teaspoon orange flower water
- 20 ml (⅔ fl oz) cane sugar syrup
- 1 teaspoon pine nuts
- handful shelled pistachios

108 SPICED
Milky Way

10 cacao beans

+

300 ml (10 fl oz) coconut water

→

Blend

+ 1 l (34 fl oz) chocolate soy milk

+ 1 pinch nutmeg

+ 1 pinch cinnamon

+ 1 l (34 fl oz) hazelnut milk

→ Blend again

→

+ 15 ice cubes

+ 5 star anise

MAKES 2.3 LITRES (78 FL OZ)
PREPARATION: 10 MINUTES

_____

- 10 cacao beans
- 300 ml (10 fl oz) coconut water
- 1 l (34 fl oz) chocolate soy milk
- 1 pinch nutmeg
- 1 pinch cinnamon
- 1 l (34 fl oz) hazelnut milk
- 15 ice cubes
- 5 star anise

109 DOUBLE CITRUS
granita

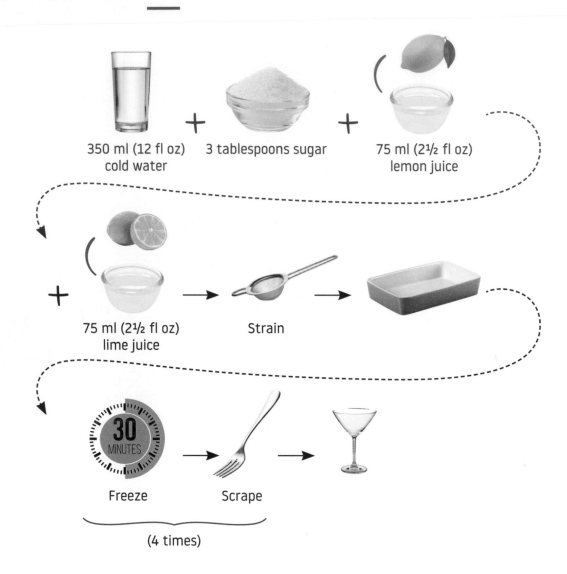

350 ml (12 fl oz)
cold water

+

3 tablespoons sugar

+

75 ml (2½ fl oz)
lemon juice

+

75 ml (2½ fl oz)
lime juice

Strain

30 MINUTES

Freeze

Scrape

(4 times)

SERVES 4
PREPARATION: 10 MINUTES
FREEZING: 2 HOURS

- 350 ml (12 fl oz) cold water
- 3 tablespoons sugar
- 75 ml (2½ fl oz) lemon juice
- 75 ml (2½ fl oz) lime juice

110 SEARED
salmon dip
—

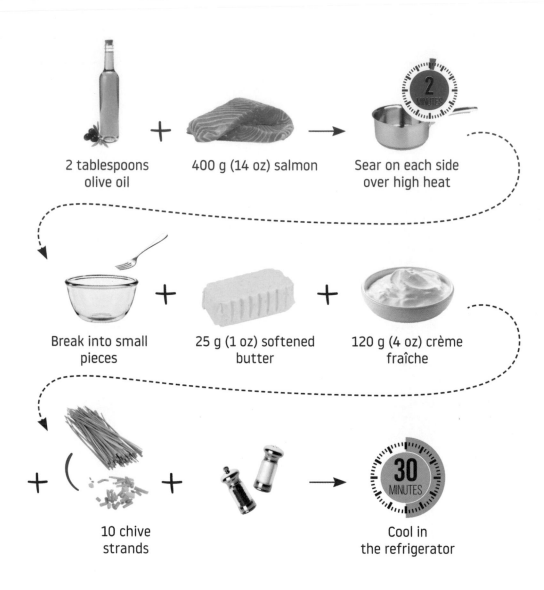

2 tablespoons
olive oil

+

400 g (14 oz) salmon

→

Sear on each side
over high heat

2 MINUTES

Break into small
pieces

+

25 g (1 oz) softened
butter

+

120 g (4 oz) crème
fraîche

+

10 chive
strands

+

→

Cool in
the refrigerator

30 MINUTES

SERVES 8
PREPARATION: 10 MINUTES
COOKING: 4 MINUTES
REFRIGERATOR: 30 MINUTES

- 2 tablespoons olive oil
- 400 g (14 oz) salmon
- 25 g (1 oz) butter
- 120 g (4 oz) crème fraîche*
- 10 chive strands, finely chopped
- salt and pepper to taste

* You can use sour cream, yoghurt or cream cheese in place of crème fraîche

111 TUNA
dip

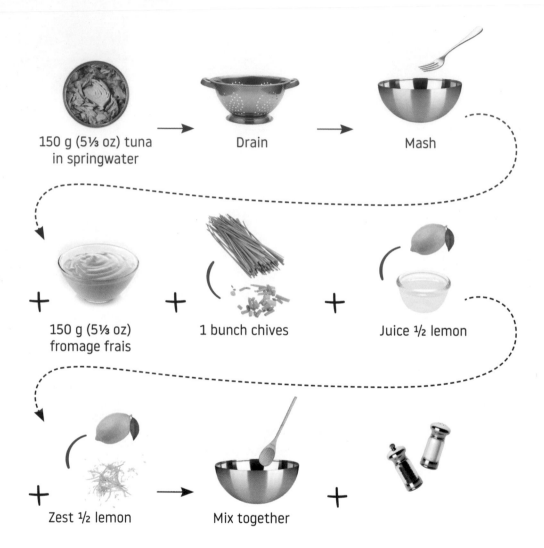

150 g (5⅓ oz) tuna
in springwater

Drain

Mash

+

150 g (5⅓ oz)
fromage frais

+

1 bunch chives

+

Juice ½ lemon

+

Zest ½ lemon

Mix together

+

SERVES 4
PREPARATION: 5 MINUTES

_____

- 150 g (5⅓ oz) tuna in spring-water
- 150 g (5⅓ oz) fromage frais*
- 1 bunch chives, chopped
- ½ lemon, juice and zest
- salt and pepper to taste

* You can use sour cream, yoghurt or cream cheese in place of fromage frais

112 PRESERVED LEMON
hommus

—

1 garlic clove + Juice 1–2 lemons + 400 g (14 oz) cooked chickpeas → Blend

+ 100 ml (3⅓ fl oz) olive oil + 1 preserved lemon + 2 tablespoons tahini +

Blend → + 1 drizzle of olive oil + Paprika

+ Coriander + Sesame seeds

SERVES 6
PREPARATION: 10 MINUTES

———————

- 1 garlic clove, peeled
- 1 or 2 lemons, juiced
- 400 g (14 oz) cooked chickpeas
- 100 ml (3⅓ fl oz) olive oil +
  1 drizzle
- 1 preserved lemon
- 2 tablespoons tahini
- salt and pepper to taste
- paprika, sesame seeds
  and coriander to garnish

113 AVOCADO PESTO
spread

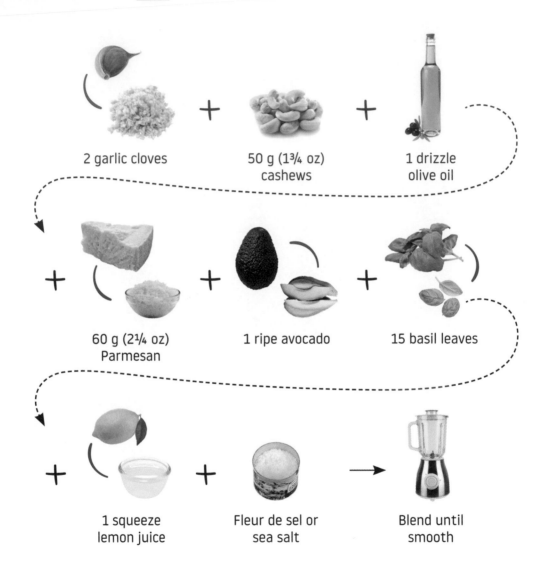

2 garlic cloves

50 g (1¾ oz) cashews

1 drizzle olive oil

60 g (2¼ oz) Parmesan

1 ripe avocado

15 basil leaves

1 squeeze lemon juice

Fleur de sel or sea salt

Blend until smooth

SERVES 4
PREPARATION: 5 MINUTES

———————

- 2 garlic cloves, peeled
- 50 g (1¾ oz) cashews
- 1 drizzle olive oil
- 60 g (2¼ oz) Parmesan, grated
- 1 ripe avocado, skinned and seeded
- 15 basil leaves
- 1 squeeze lemon juice
- fleur de sel or sea salt

114 TUNA SURPRISE
eggs

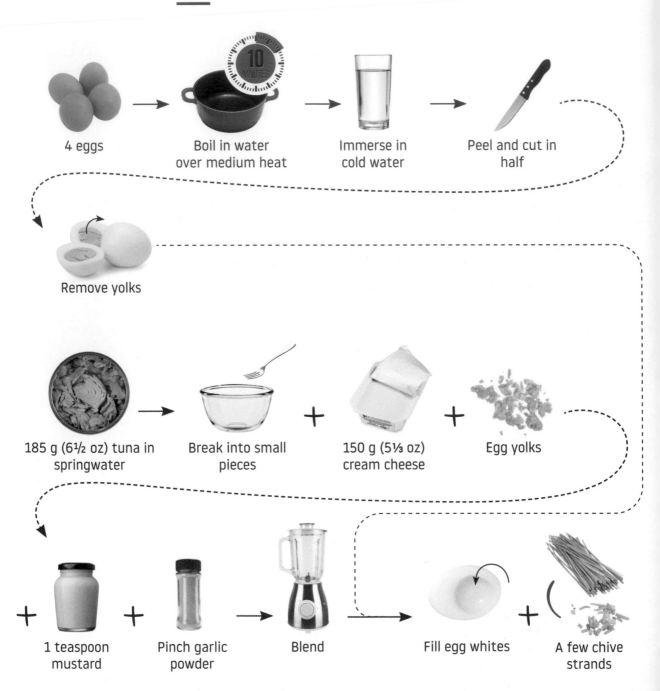

4 eggs → Boil in water over medium heat (10 MINUTES) → Immerse in cold water → Peel and cut in half

Remove yolks

185 g (6½ oz) tuna in springwater → Break into small pieces + 150 g (5⅓ oz) cream cheese + Egg yolks

+ 1 teaspoon mustard + Pinch garlic powder → Blend → Fill egg whites + A few chive strands

SERVES 4
PREPARATION: 15 MINUTES
COOKING: 10 MINUTES

———————————

• 4 eggs, boiled
• 185 g (6½ oz) tuna in spring-
  water, undrained
• 150 g (5⅓ oz) cream cheese
• 1 teaspoon mustard
• pinch garlic powder
• a few chive strands, chopped

115 MINI HAM AND
cheese rolls
—

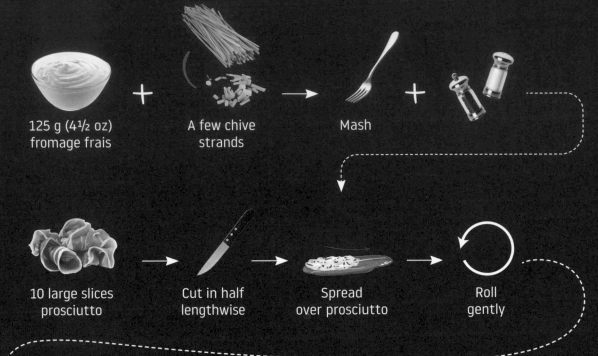

125 g (4½ oz)
fromage frais

+

A few chive
strands

→ Mash +

10 large slices
prosciutto

→ Cut in half
lengthwise

→ Spread
over prosciutto

→ Roll
gently

30
MINUTES

Refrigerate

MAKES 20 ROLLS
PREPARATION: 10 MINUTES
REFRIGERATION: 30 MINUTES

———————

• 125 g (4½ oz) fromage frais*
• a few chive strands, chopped
• salt and pepper to taste
• 10 large slices prosciutto

* You can use sour cream,
yoghurt or cream cheese in place
of fromage frais

116 AVOCADO
and turkey pops
—

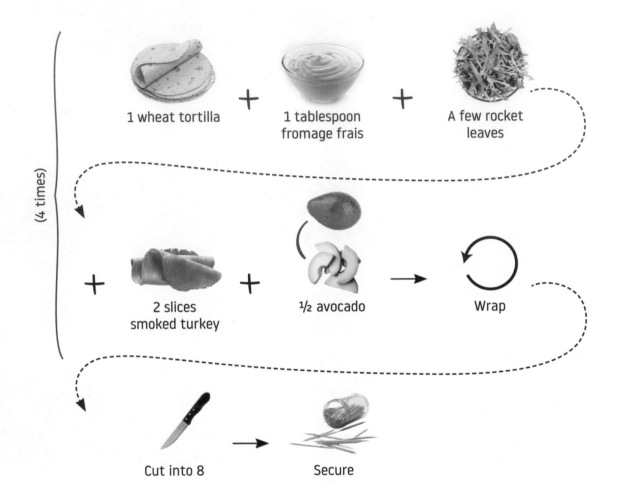

(4 times)

1 wheat tortilla + 1 tablespoon fromage frais + A few rocket leaves

+ 2 slices smoked turkey + ½ avocado → Wrap

Cut into 8 → Secure

SERVES 4
PREPARATION: 15 MINUTES

_____

• 1 wheat tortilla
• 1 tablespoon fromage frais*
• a few rocket leaves
• 2 slices smoked turkey
• ½ avocado, peeled and diced

* You can use sour cream,
yoghurt or cream cheese in place
of fromage frais

117 DEVILS
on horseback

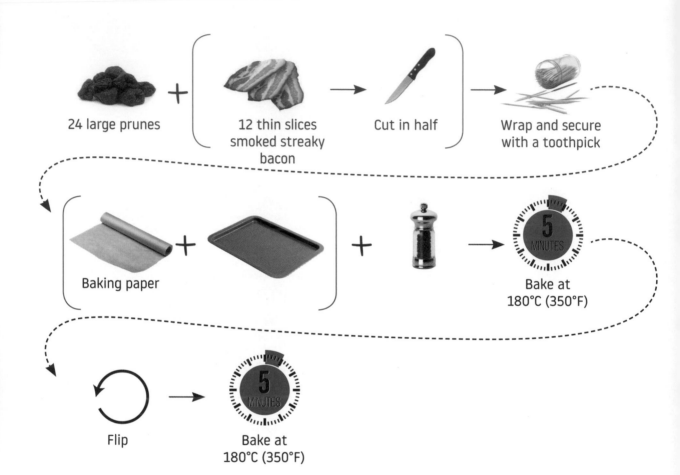

24 large prunes + 12 thin slices smoked streaky bacon → Cut in half → Wrap and secure with a toothpick

Baking paper + → Bake at 180°C (350°F) 5 MINUTES

Flip → Bake at 180°C (350°F) 5 MINUTES

SERVES 6
PREPARATION: 15 MINUTES
COOKING: 10 MINUTES

• 24 large pitted prunes
• 12 thin slices smoked streaky
  bacon, halved
• pepper to taste

118 CRUMBED PRAWN
skewers

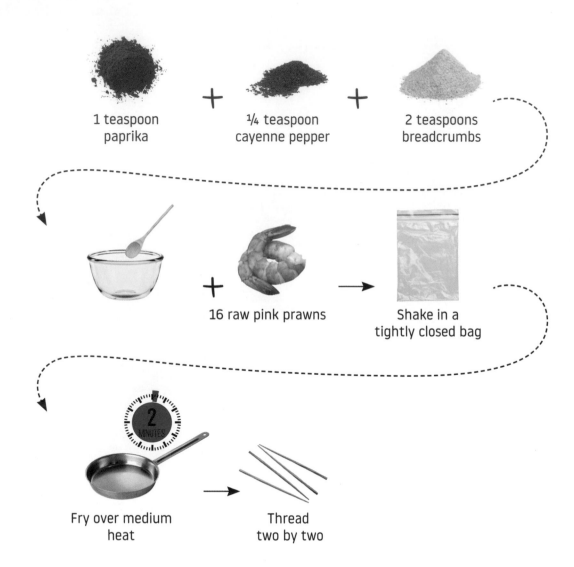

1 teaspoon
paprika

+

¼ teaspoon
cayenne pepper

+

2 teaspoons
breadcrumbs

16 raw pink prawns

Shake in a
tightly closed bag

Fry over medium
heat

Thread
two by two

SERVES 4
PREPARATION: 15 MINUTES
COOKING: 2 MINUTES

- 1 teaspoon paprika
- ¼ teaspoon cayenne pepper
- 2 teaspoons breadcrumbs
- 16 raw pink prawns, shelled and deveined, tails intact

119 SEEDED
cheese balls

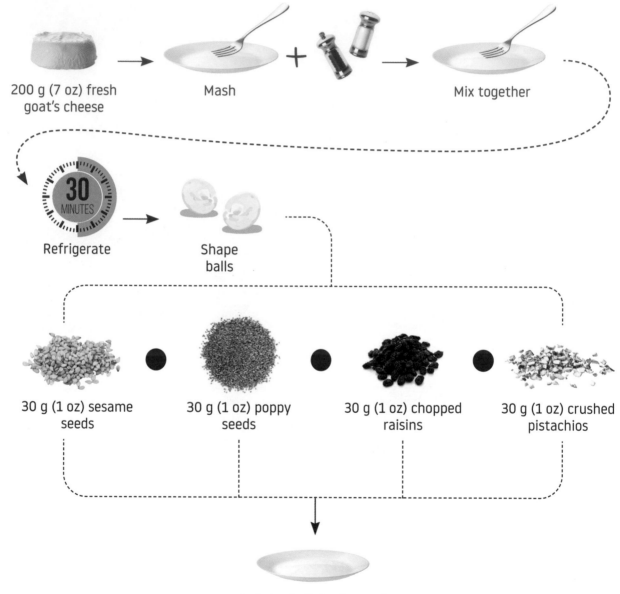

200 g (7 oz) fresh goat's cheese

Mash

Mix together

30 MINUTES

Refrigerate

Shape balls

30 g (1 oz) sesame seeds

30 g (1 oz) poppy seeds

30 g (1 oz) chopped raisins

30 g (1 oz) crushed pistachios

Roll the balls in the seeds and dried fruit

SERVES 4
PREPARATION: 15 MINUTES
REFRIGERATION: 30 MINUTES

_____

• 200 g (7 oz) fresh goat's cheese
• salt and pepper to taste
• 30 g (1 oz) sesame seeds
• 30 g (1 oz) poppy seeds
• 30 g (1 oz) raisins
• 30 g (1 oz) crushed pistachios

120 PROSCIUTTO AND BASIL
roasted peaches

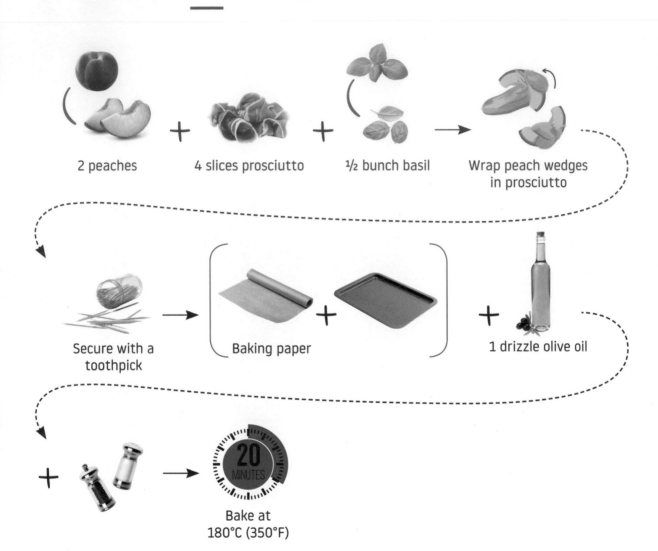

2 peaches + 4 slices prosciutto + ½ bunch basil → Wrap peach wedges in prosciutto

Secure with a toothpick → Baking paper + [baking tray] + 1 drizzle olive oil

+ [salt and pepper] → 20 MINUTES

Bake at 180°C (350°F)

SERVES 4
PREPARATION: 15 MINUTES
COOKING: 20 MINUTES

- 2 peaches, seeded and cut into
  wedges
- 4 slices prosciutto
- ½ bunch basil
- 1 drizzle olive oil
- salt and pepper to taste

121 MOZZARELLA,
olive and tomato pops
—

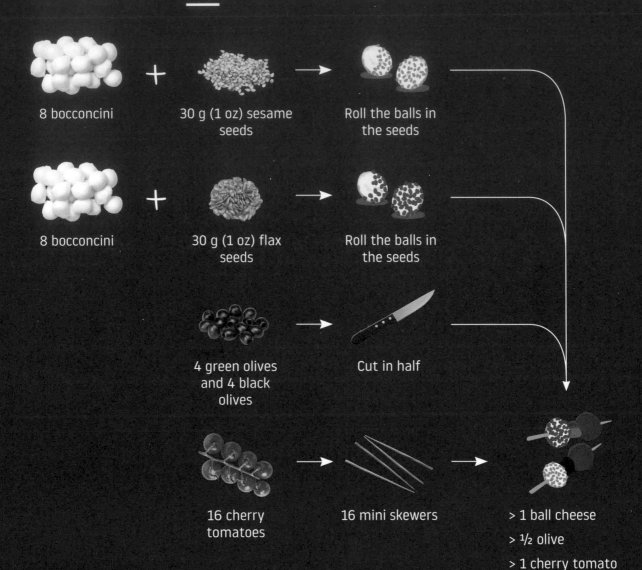

8 bocconcini + 30 g (1 oz) sesame seeds → Roll the balls in the seeds

8 bocconcini + 30 g (1 oz) flax seeds → Roll the balls in the seeds

4 green olives and 4 black olives → Cut in half

16 cherry tomatoes → 16 mini skewers →

> 1 ball cheese
> ½ olive
> 1 cherry tomato

SERVES 4
PREPARATION: 10 MINUTES

• 16 bocconcini
• 30 g (1 oz) sesame seeds
• 30 g (1 oz) flax seeds
• 4 green olives, halved
• 4 black olives, halved
• 16 cherry tomatoes

122 VEGETABLE *chips*

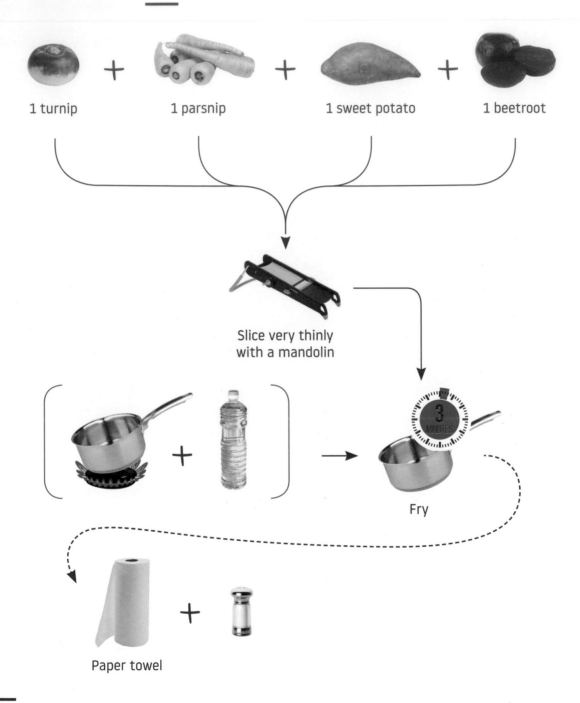

1 turnip + 1 parsnip + 1 sweet potato + 1 beetroot

Slice very thinly
with a mandolin

+

→ 3 MINUTES

Fry

Paper towel +

SERVES 4
PREPARATION: 10 MINUTES
COOKING: 3 MINUTES

———————————

• 1 turnip, thinly sliced
• 1 parsnip, thinly sliced
• 1 sweet potato, thinly sliced
• 1 beetroot, thinly sliced
• oil for frying
• salt to taste

123 SPICY *chickpeas*

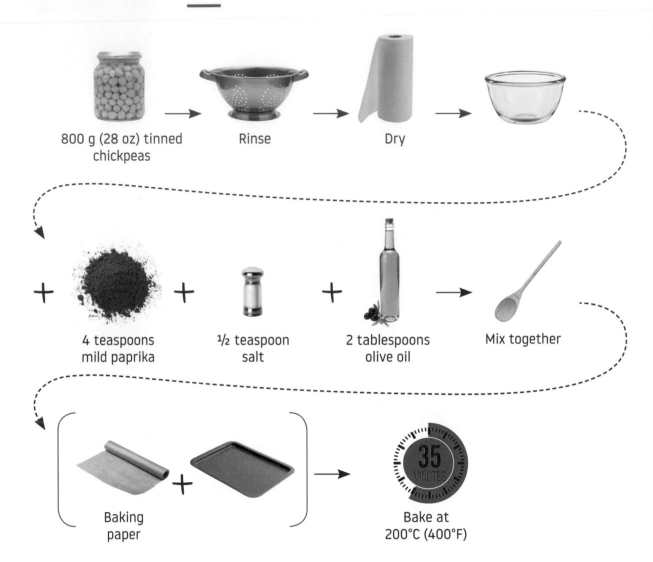

800 g (28 oz) tinned chickpeas → Rinse → Dry →

+ 4 teaspoons mild paprika + ½ teaspoon salt + 2 tablespoons olive oil → Mix together

[Baking paper +] → **35** MINUTES — Bake at 200°C (400°F)

SERVES 4 TO 6
PREPARATION: 5 MINUTES
COOKING: 35 MINUTES

——————————

• 800 g (28 oz) tinned chickpeas
• 4 teaspoons mild paprika
• ½ teaspoon salt
• 2 tablespoons olive oil

124 SESAME crackers

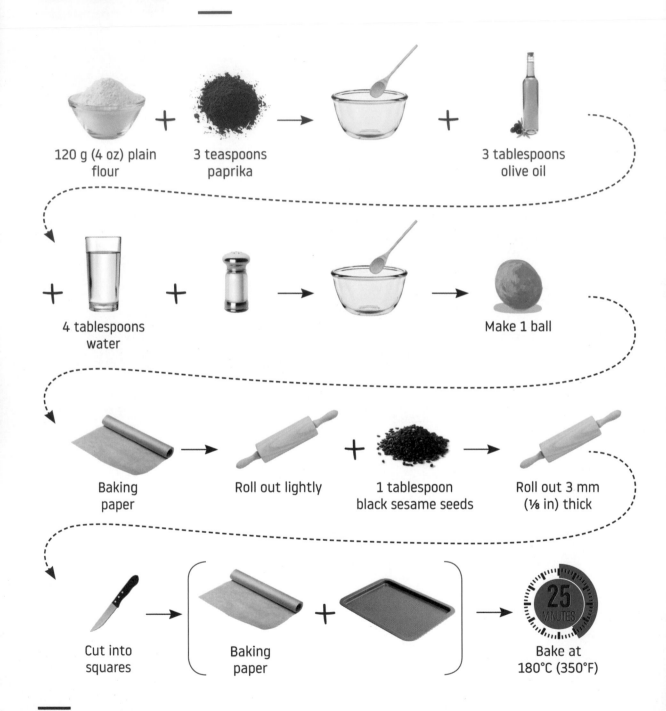

120 g (4 oz) plain flour + 3 teaspoons paprika →

+ 3 tablespoons olive oil

+ 4 tablespoons water + →

Make 1 ball

Baking paper → Roll out lightly + 1 tablespoon black sesame seeds → Roll out 3 mm (⅛ in) thick

Cut into squares → Baking paper + → Bake at 180°C (350°F) 25 MINUTES

SERVES 8
PREPARATION: 15 MINUTES
COOKING: 25 MINUTES

_____

- 120 g (4 oz) plain flour
- 3 teaspoons hot paprika
- 2 tablespoons olive oil
- 4 tablespoons water
- salt to taste
- 1 tablespoon black sesame seeds

125 CHORIZO RICOTTA
pizza twists

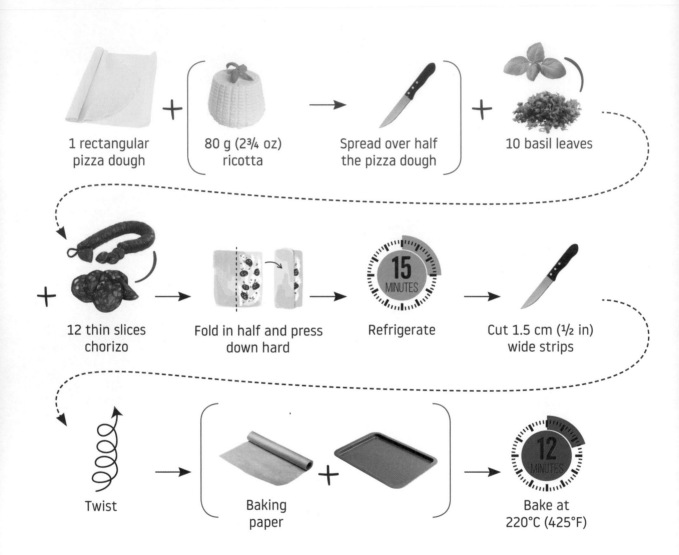

1 rectangular
pizza dough

+

80 g (2¾ oz)
ricotta

Spread over half
the pizza dough

+

10 basil leaves

+

12 thin slices
chorizo

Fold in half and press
down hard

Refrigerate
15 MINUTES

Cut 1.5 cm (½ in)
wide strips

Twist

Baking
paper

+

Bake at
220°C (425°F)
12 MINUTES

SERVES 6
PREPARATION: 15 MINUTES
REFRIGERATION: 15 MINUTES
COOKING: 12 MINUTES

• 1 rectangular pre-rolled pizza dough
• 80 g (2¾ oz) ricotta
• 10 basil leaves, chopped
• 12 thin slices chorizo

126 HONEYED GOAT'S CHEESE
parcels

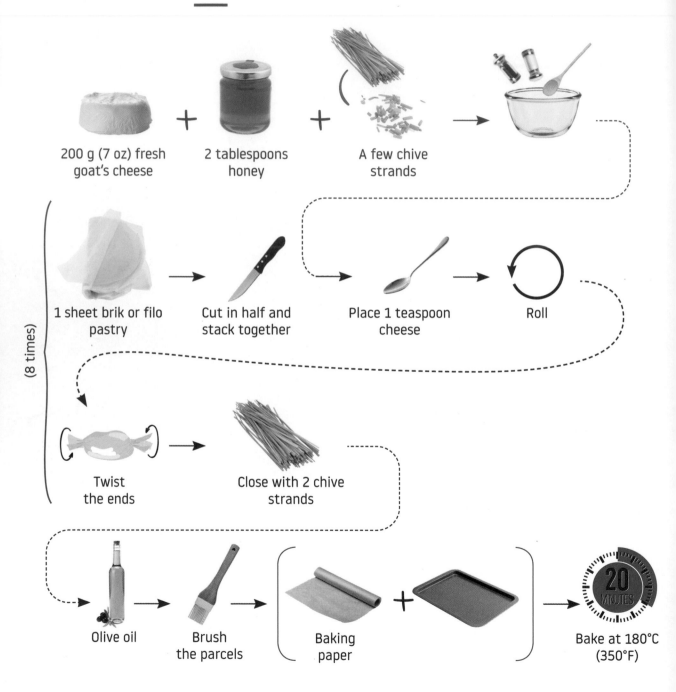

200 g (7 oz) fresh
goat's cheese

+

2 tablespoons
honey

+

A few chive
strands

→

(8 times)

1 sheet brik or filo
pastry

→

Cut in half and
stack together

→

Place 1 teaspoon
cheese

→

Roll

Twist
the ends

→

Close with 2 chive
strands

Olive oil

→

Brush
the parcels

→

Baking
paper

+

Bake at 180°C
(350°F)

20 MINUTES

SERVES 4
PREPARATION: 10 MINUTES
COOKING: 20 MINUTES

———————

• 200 g (7 oz) fresh goat's cheese
• 2 tablespoons honey
• a few chive strands, finely
  chopped + to garnish
• salt and pepper to taste
• 8 sheets brik or filo pastry
• olive oil

127 EGGPLANT MOZZARELLA
mini pizzas

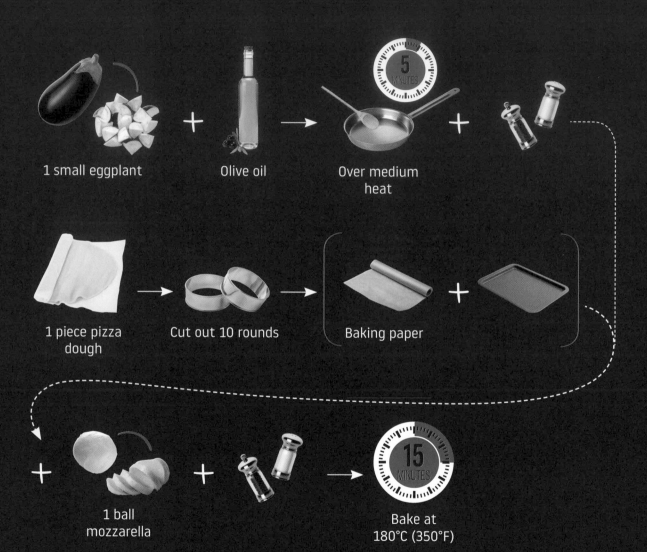

1 small eggplant + Olive oil → Over medium heat + 5 MINUTES

1 piece pizza dough → Cut out 10 rounds → Baking paper +

+ 1 ball mozzarella + → Bake at 180°C (350°F) 15 MINUTES

SERVES 10
PREPARATION: 15 MINUTES
COOKING: 20 MINUTES

• 1 small eggplant, diced
• olive oil
• salt and pepper to taste
• 1 piece pizza dough
• 1 ball mozzarella, sliced

128 CAULIFLOWER
bites

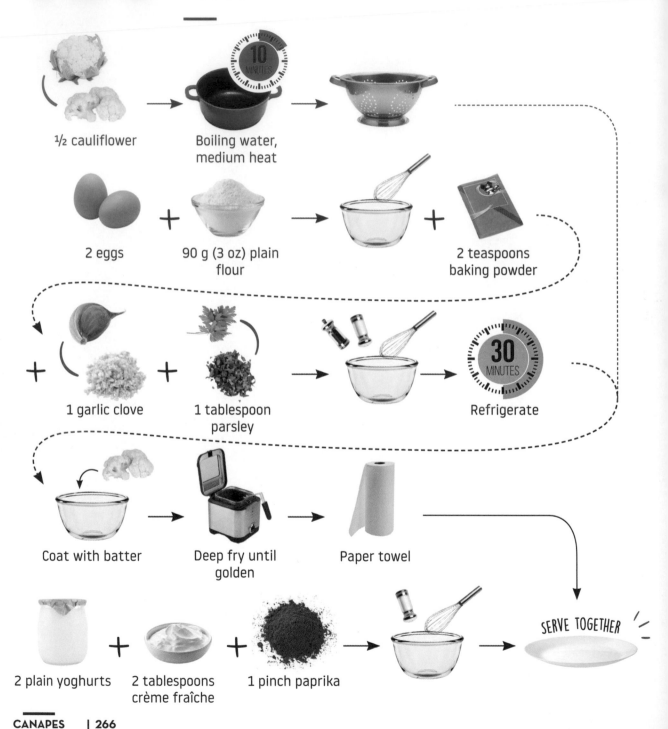

½ cauliflower

Boiling water, medium heat

10 MINUTES

2 eggs

+

90 g (3 oz) plain flour

+

2 teaspoons baking powder

+

1 garlic clove

+

1 tablespoon parsley

30 MINUTES

Refrigerate

Coat with batter

Deep fry until golden

Paper towel

2 plain yoghurts

+

2 tablespoons crème fraîche

+

1 pinch paprika

SERVE TOGETHER

SERVES 4
PREPARATION: 25 MINUTES
REFRIGERATION: 30 MINUTES
COOKING: 25 MINUTES

——————————

- ½ cauliflower, cut into small florets
- 2 eggs
- 90 g (3 oz) plain flour
- 2 teaspoons baking powder
- 1 garlic clove, peeled and crushed
- 1 tablespoon parsley, finely chopped
- salt and pepper to taste
- oil for frying
- 2 plain yoghurts
- 2 tablespoons crème fraîche*
- 1 pinch paprika

* You can use sour cream, yoghurt or cream cheese in place of crème fraîche

129 COD *fritters*

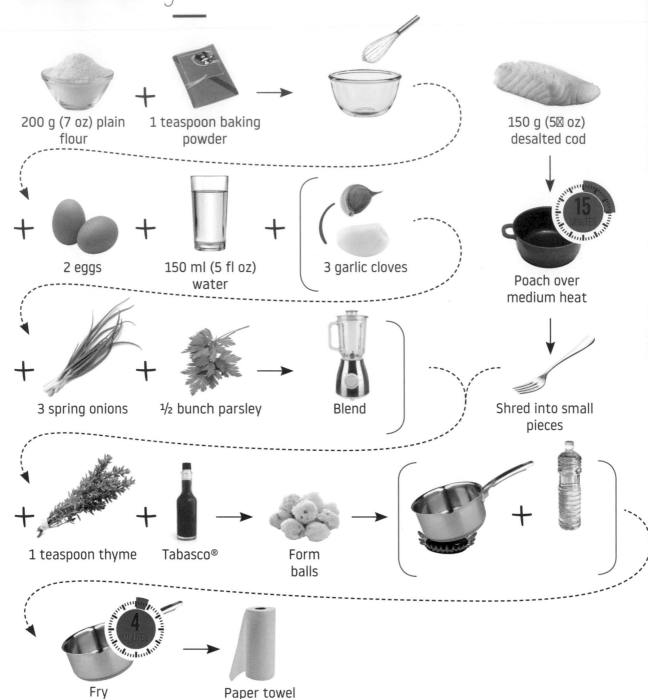

200 g (7 oz) plain flour + 1 teaspoon baking powder →

150 g (5⊠ oz) desalted cod

2 eggs + 150 ml (5 fl oz) water + 3 garlic cloves

Poach over medium heat

15 MINUTES

3 spring onions + ½ bunch parsley → Blend

Shred into small pieces

1 teaspoon thyme + Tabasco® → Form balls →

Fry

4 MINUTES

Paper towel

SERVES 4
PREPARATION: 15 MINUTES
COOKING: 19 MINUTES

- 150 g (5⅓ oz) desalted cod
- 200 g (7 oz) plain flour
- 1 teaspoon baking powder
- 2 eggs
- 150 ml (5 fl oz) water
- 3 garlic cloves, peeled
- 3 spring onions, chopped
- ½ bunch parsley
- 1 teaspoon fresh thyme
- Tabasco®
- oil for frying

130 OVEN-BAKED *falafels*

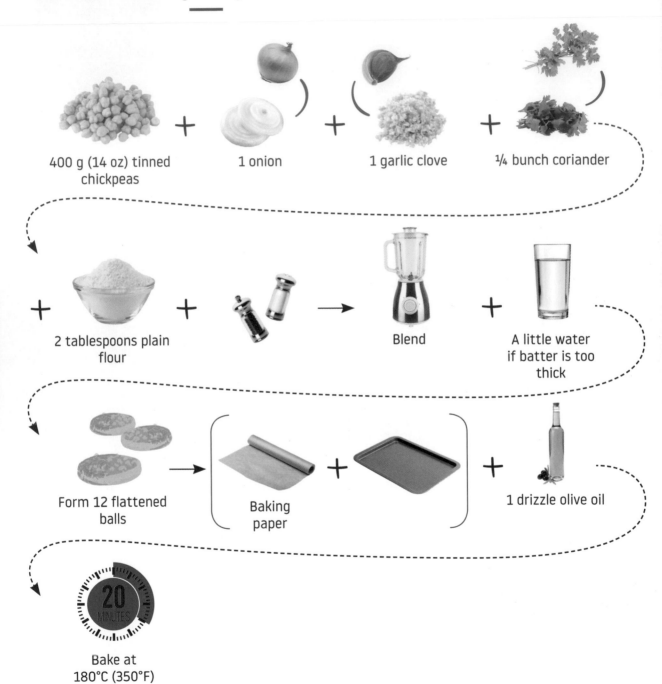

400 g (14 oz) tinned chickpeas

+

1 onion

+

1 garlic clove

+

¼ bunch coriander

+

2 tablespoons plain flour

+

→ Blend

+

A little water if batter is too thick

Form 12 flattened balls

→ Baking paper + (baking tray)

+

1 drizzle olive oil

20 MINUTES

Bake at 180°C (350°F)

SERVES 4
PREPARATION: 10 MINUTES
COOKING: 20 MINUTES

- 400 g (14 oz) tinned chickpeas
- 1 onion, peeled and sliced
- 1 garlic clove, peeled
- ¼ bunch coriander
- 2 tablespoons plain flour
- salt and pepper to taste
- 1 drizzle olive oil

131 MINI BASIL AND GOAT'S
cheese puffs

120 ml (4 fl oz) water

+

40 g (1⅓ oz) butter

+

Bring to the boil

5 MINUTES

Off the heat

+

80 g (2¾ oz) plain flour

Mix to form a smooth batter

Allow to cool slightly

+

2 eggs

+

+

80 g (3 oz) fresh goat's cheese

+

4 basil leaves

Place spoonfuls onto tray

Bake at 180°C (350°F)

25 MINUTES

5 MINUTES

Allow to cool with oven door open

MAKES 24 CHEESE PUFFS
PREPARATION: 15 MINUTES
COOKING: 30 MINUTES
COOLING: 5 MINUTES

- 120 ml (4 fl oz) water
- 40 g (1⅓ oz) butter
- salt to taste
- 80 g (2¾ oz) plain flour
- 2 eggs, beaten
- pepper to taste
- 80 g (2¾ oz) fresh goat's cheese
- 4 basil leaves, chopped

132 SPINACH ROQUEFORT
mini muffins
—

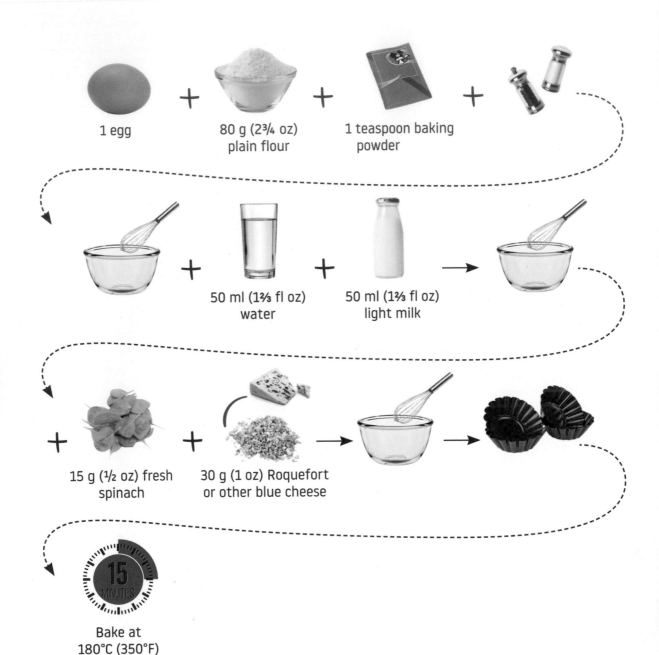

1 egg + 80 g (2¾ oz) plain flour + 1 teaspoon baking powder +

+ 50 ml (1⅔ fl oz) water + 50 ml (1⅔ fl oz) light milk →

+ 15 g (½ oz) fresh spinach + 30 g (1 oz) Roquefort or other blue cheese → →

15 MINUTES

Bake at 180℃ (350°F)

MAKES 18 MINI MUFFINS
PREPARATION: 15 MINUTES
COOKING: 15 MINUTES

———————————————

- 1 egg
- 80g (2¾ oz) plain flour
- 1 teaspoon baking powder
- salt and pepper to taste
- 50 ml (1⅔ fl oz) water
- 50 ml (1⅔ fl oz) light milk
- 15 g (½ oz) fresh spinach
- 30 g (1 oz) Roquefort or other blue cheese

133 CHICKEN
nuggets

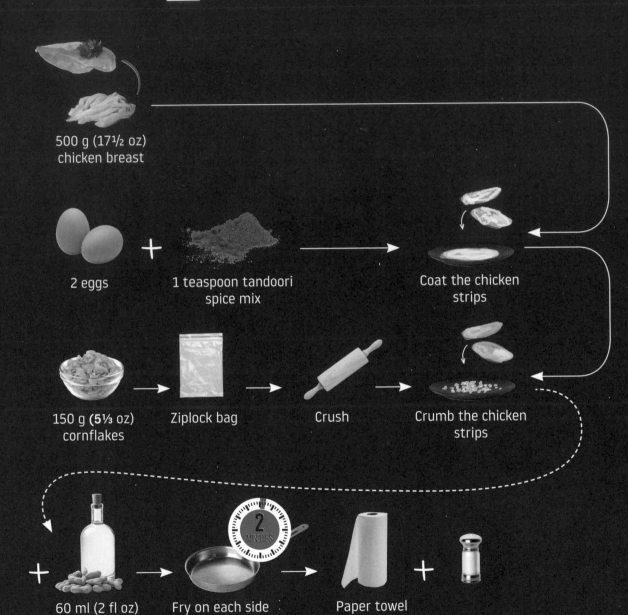

500 g (17½ oz)
chicken breast

2 eggs

+

1 teaspoon tandoori
spice mix

Coat the chicken
strips

150 g (5⅓ oz)
cornflakes

Ziplock bag

Crush

Crumb the chicken
strips

+

60 ml (2 fl oz)
peanut oil

Fry on each side
over high heat

2 MINUTES

Paper towel

+

SERVES 4
PREPARATION: 20 MINUTES
COOKING: 4 MINUTES

———————————

- 500 g (17½ oz) skinless chicken breast, cut into strips
- 2 eggs
- 1 teaspoon tandoori spice mix
- 150 g (5⅓ oz) cornflakes
- 60 ml (2 fl oz) peanut oil
- salt to taste

134 TOMATO AND HAM
crostinis

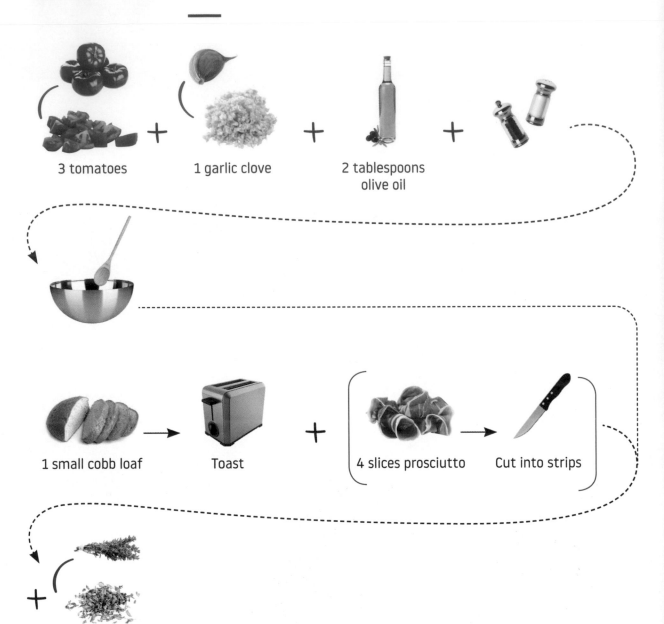

3 tomatoes + 1 garlic clove + 2 tablespoons olive oil +

1 small cobb loaf → Toast + 4 slices prosciutto → Cut into strips

+ ½ teaspoon fresh thyme

MAKES 10 CROSTINIS
PREPARATION: 15 MINUTES

────────────

- 3 tomatoes, diced
- 1 garlic clove, crushed
- 2 tablespoons olive oil
- salt and pepper to taste
- 1 small cobb loaf, sliced
- 4 slices prosciutto, cut into strips
- ½ teaspoon fresh thyme

135 SMOKED
trout blinis

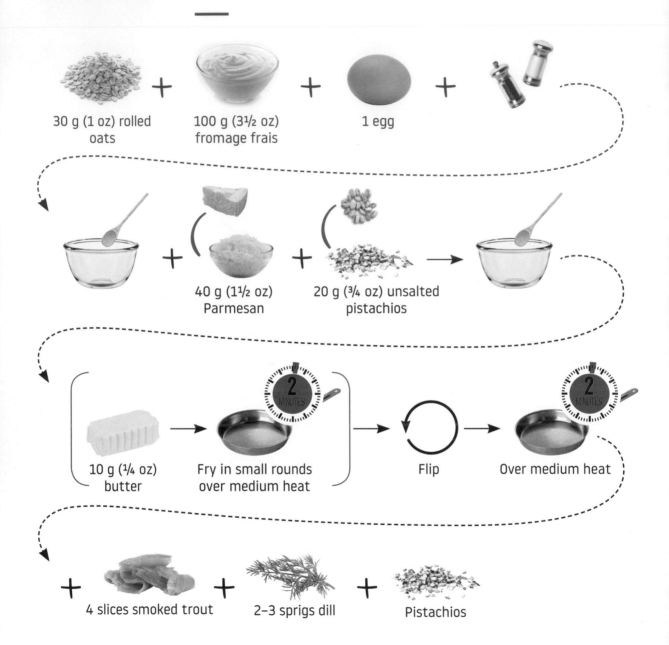

30 g (1 oz) rolled oats

100 g (3½ oz) fromage frais

1 egg

40 g (1½ oz) Parmesan

20 g (¾ oz) unsalted pistachios

10 g (¼ oz) butter

Fry in small rounds over medium heat

2 MINUTES

Flip

Over medium heat

2 MINUTES

4 slices smoked trout

2–3 sprigs dill

Pistachios

SERVES 4
PREPARATION: 10 MINUTES
COOKING: 10 MINUTES

- 30 g (1 oz) rolled oats
- 100 g (3½ oz) fromage frais*
- 1 egg
- salt and pepper to taste
- 40 g (1½ oz) Parmesan, grated
- 20 g (¾ oz) unsalted pistachios, finely chopped + extra to decorate
- 10 g (¼ oz) butter
- 4 slices smoked trout, cut into small piece
- 2–3 sprigs dill

* You can use sour cream, yoghurt or cream cheese in place of fromage frais

136 FRIED PRAWN
dumplings

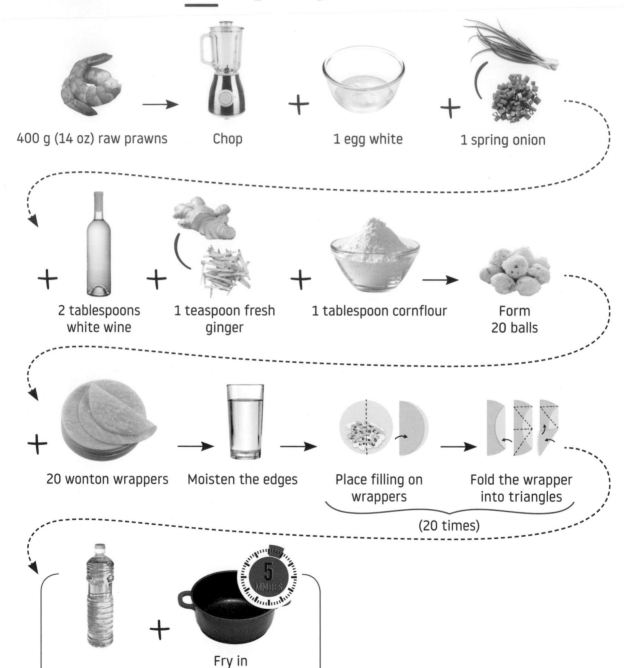

400 g (14 oz) raw prawns → Chop + 1 egg white + 1 spring onion

+ 2 tablespoons white wine + 1 teaspoon fresh ginger + 1 tablespoon cornflour → Form 20 balls

+ 20 wonton wrappers → Moisten the edges → Place filling on wrappers → Fold the wrapper into triangles

(20 times)

+ **5 MINUTES** Fry in two batches

SERVES 4
PREPARATION: 25 MINUTES
COOKING: 10 MINUTES

- 400 g (14 oz) prawns, peeled and deveined
- 1 egg white, beaten
- 1 spring onion, chopped
- 2 tablespoons white wine
- 1 teaspoon fresh ginger, grated
- 1 tablespoon cornflour
- 20 wonton wrappers
- oil for frying

137 BACON AND CHEDDAR
mini quiches

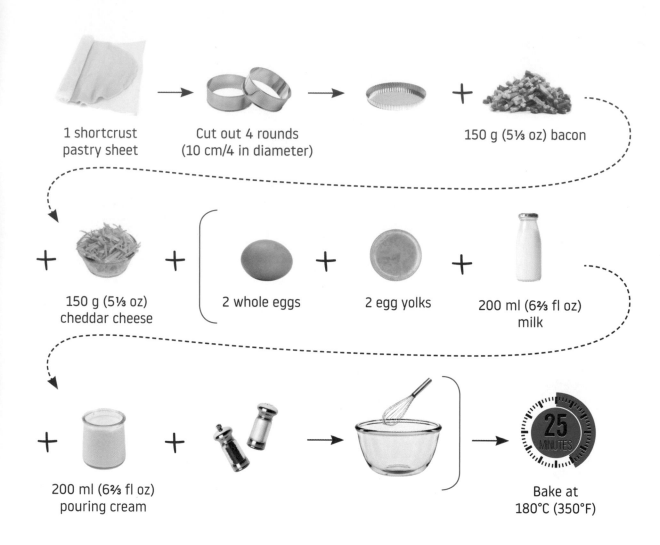

1 shortcrust pastry sheet

Cut out 4 rounds (10 cm/4 in diameter)

150 g (5⅓ oz) bacon

150 g (5⅓ oz) cheddar cheese

2 whole eggs

2 egg yolks

200 ml (6⅔ fl oz) milk

200 ml (6⅔ fl oz) pouring cream

Bake at 180°C (350°F)

25 MINUTES

SERVES 4
PREPARATION: 15 MINUTES
COOKING: 25 MINUTES

_____

- 1 shortcrust pastry sheet
- 150 g (5⅓ oz) bacon, diced
- 150 g (5⅓ oz) cheddar cheese, grated
- 2 eggs + 2 yolks
- 200 ml (6⅔ fl oz) milk
- 200 ml (6⅔ fl oz) pouring cream
- salt and pepper to taste

138 SALMON AND APPLE
tartare
—

250 g (9 oz) salmon + 2 Granny Smith apples + 1 lime, zested + Juice 1 lime

+ 4 tablespoons olive oil + ½ bunch chives → +

Divide into 6 small glasses + 2 tablespoons sesame seeds

SERVES 6
PREPARATION: 10 MINUTES

———————

- 250 g (9 oz) salmon, skinned and diced
- 2 Granny Smith apples, diced
- 1 lime, zested and juiced
- 4 tablespoons olive oil
- ½ bunch chives, finely chopped
- salt and pepper to taste
- 2 tablespoons sesame seeds

139 CARROT AND COCONUT
gazpacho

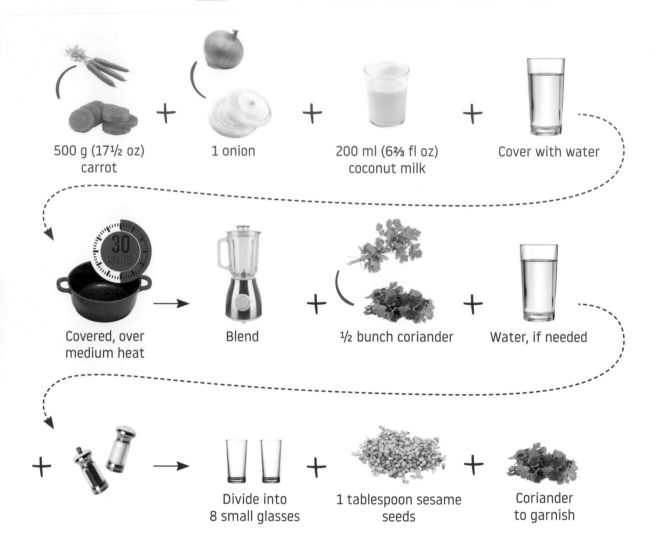

500 g (17½ oz) carrot

+

1 onion

+

200 ml (6⅔ fl oz) coconut milk

+

Cover with water

Covered, over medium heat

→

Blend

+

½ bunch coriander

+

Water, if needed

+

→

Divide into 8 small glasses

+

1 tablespoon sesame seeds

+

Coriander to garnish

SERVES 8
PREPARATION: 15 MINUTES
COOKING: 30 MINUTES

———————

- 500 g (17½ oz) carrot, sliced
- 1 onion, peeled and chopped
- 200 ml (6⅔ fl oz) coconut milk
- ½ bunch coriander + extra to garnish
- salt and pepper to taste
- 1 tablespoon sesame seeds

140 MOZZARELLA
and prosciutto pizza

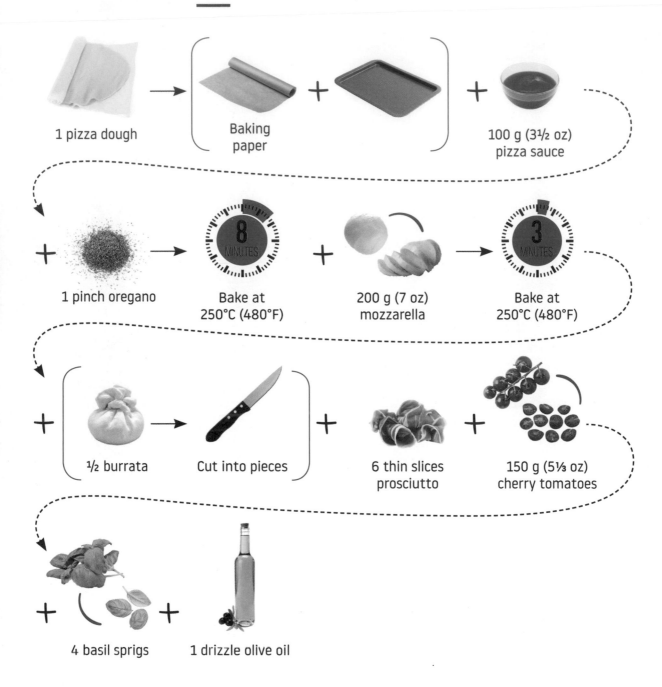

1 pizza dough → Baking paper + [baking tray] + 100 g (3½ oz) pizza sauce

+ 1 pinch oregano → Bake at 250°C (480°F) **8 MINUTES** + 200 g (7 oz) mozzarella → Bake at 250°C (480°F) **3 MINUTES**

+ ½ burrata → Cut into pieces + 6 thin slices prosciutto + 150 g (5⅓ oz) cherry tomatoes

+ 4 basil sprigs + 1 drizzle olive oil

SERVES 4
PREPARATION: 30 MINUTES
COOKING: 11 MINUTES

———————

• 1 pizza dough
• 100 g (3½ oz) pizza sauce
• 1 pinch oregano
• 200 g (7 oz) mozzarella, sliced
• ½ burrata, cut into pieces
• 6 thin slices prosciutto
• 150 g (5⅓ oz) cherry tomatoes,
  halved
• 4 basil sprigs
• 1 drizzle olive oil

141 PESTO, MOZZARELLA
and zucchini tart

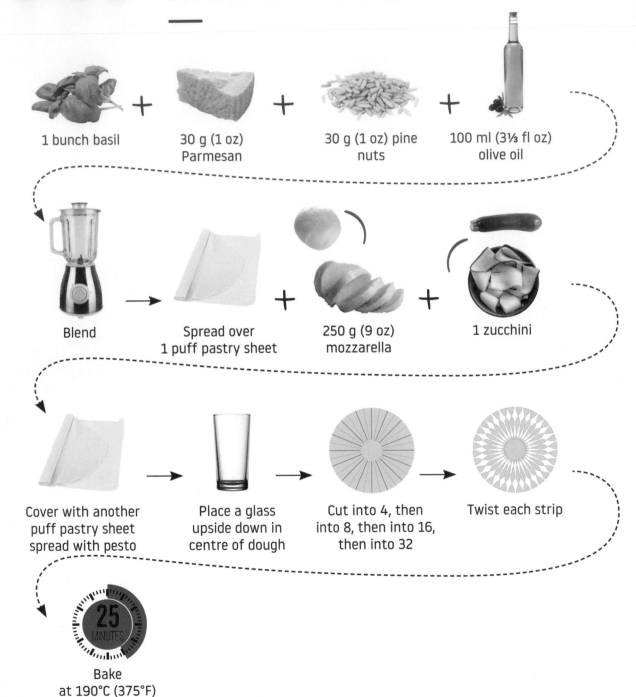

1 bunch basil + 30 g (1 oz) Parmesan + 30 g (1 oz) pine nuts + 100 ml (3⅓ fl oz) olive oil

Blend → Spread over 1 puff pastry sheet + 250 g (9 oz) mozzarella + 1 zucchini

Cover with another puff pastry sheet spread with pesto → Place a glass upside down in centre of dough → Cut into 4, then into 8, then into 16, then into 32 → Twist each strip

25 MINUTES

Bake at 190°C (375°F)

SERVES 6
PREPARATION: 20 MINUTES
COOKING: 25 MINUTES

———————————

- 1 bunch basil
- 30 g (1 oz) Parmesan, grated
- 30 g (1 oz) pine nuts
- 100 ml (3⅓ fl oz) olive oil
- 2 puff pastry sheets
- 250 g (9 oz) mozzarella, sliced
- 1 zucchini, cut into thin strips
  lengthwise

142 OLIVE
flat bread
—

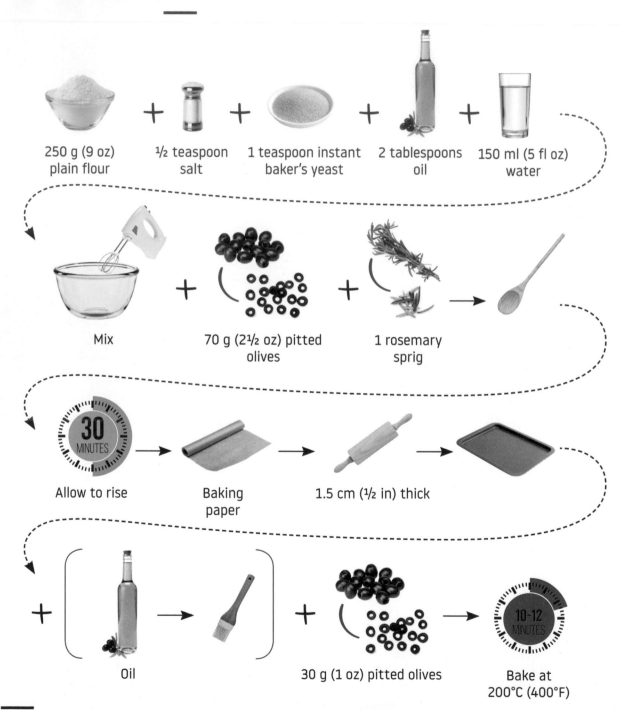

250 g (9 oz) plain flour

+

½ teaspoon salt

+

1 teaspoon instant baker's yeast

+

2 tablespoons oil

+

150 ml (5 fl oz) water

Mix

+

70 g (2½ oz) pitted olives

+

1 rosemary sprig

→

30 MINUTES
Allow to rise

→

Baking paper

→

1.5 cm (½ in) thick

→

+

Oil

+

30 g (1 oz) pitted olives

→

10–12 MINUTES
Bake at 200°C (400°F)

SERVES 4
PREPARATION: 15 MINUTES
RESTING: 30 MINUTES
COOKING: 10–12 MINUTES

- 250 g (9 oz) plain flour
- ½ teaspoon salt
- 1 teaspoon instant baker's yeast
- 2 tablespoons oil
- 150 ml (5 fl oz) water
- 100 g (3½ oz) pitted olives, sliced
- 1 rosemary sprig

143 FOCCACIA
with cherry tomatoes

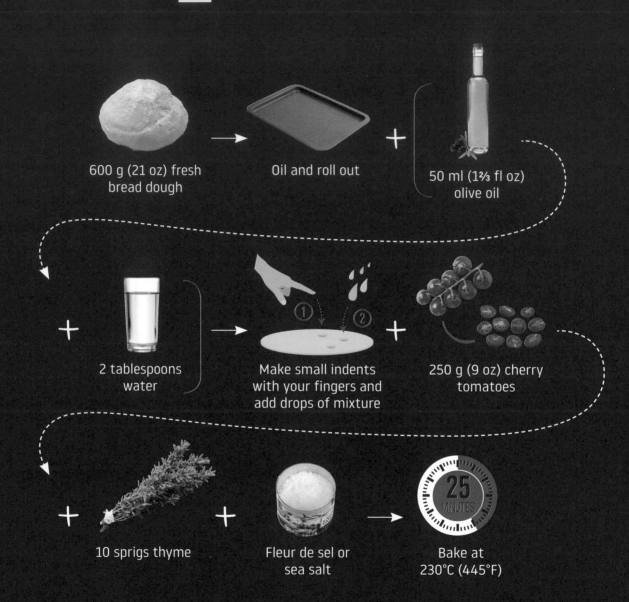

600 g (21 oz) fresh
bread dough

Oil and roll out

50 ml (1⅔ fl oz)
olive oil

2 tablespoons
water

Make small indents
with your fingers and
add drops of mixture

250 g (9 oz) cherry
tomatoes

10 sprigs thyme

Fleur de sel or
sea salt

25 MINUTES

Bake at
230°C (445°F)

SERVES 6
PREPARATION: 15 MINUTES
COOKING: 25 MINUTES

———————

- 600 g (21 oz) fresh bread dough
- 50 ml (1⅔ fl oz) olive oil
- 2 tablespoons water
- 250 g (9 oz) cherry tomatoes, halved
- 10 sprigs thyme
- Fleur de sel or sea salt

144 GARLIC
bread

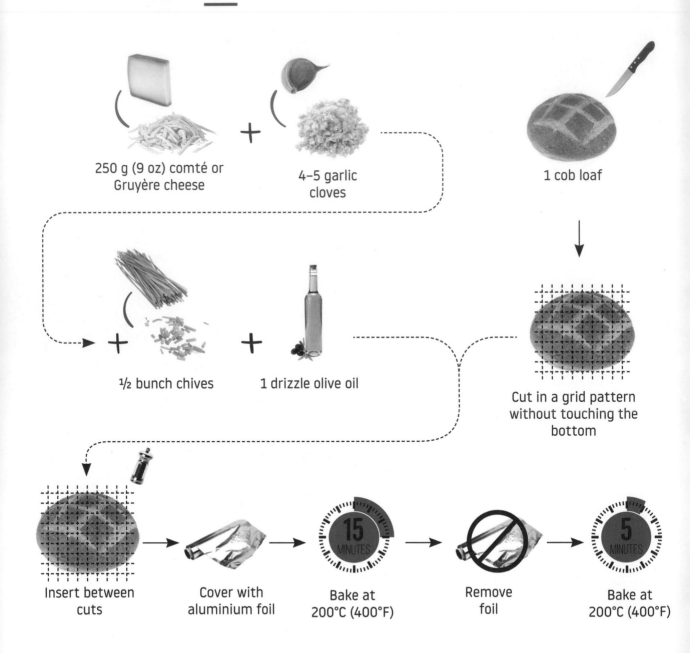

250 g (9 oz) comté or
Gruyère cheese

+

4–5 garlic
cloves

1 cob loaf

½ bunch chives

+

1 drizzle olive oil

Cut in a grid pattern
without touching the
bottom

Insert between
cuts

Cover with
aluminium foil

Bake at
200°C (400°F)

15 MINUTES

Remove
foil

Bake at
200°C (400°F)

5 MINUTES

SERVES 6
PREPARATION: 20 MINUTES
COOKING: 20 MINUTES

- 250 g (9 oz) comté or Gruyère cheese, grated
- 4–5 garlic cloves, crushed
- 1 cob loaf
- ½ bunch chives, chopped
- 1 drizzle olive oil
- pepper to taste

145 MUSHROOM
hedgehog bread
—

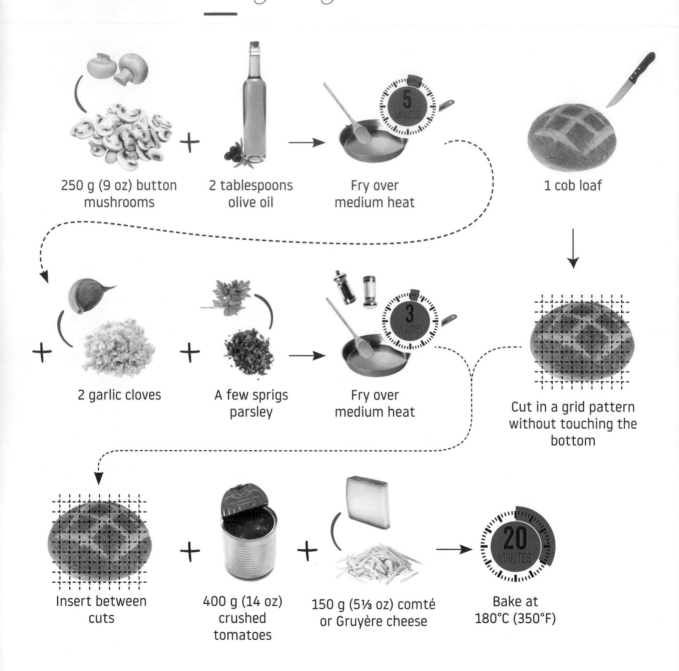

250 g (9 oz) button mushrooms

+

2 tablespoons olive oil

Fry over medium heat

5 MINUTES

1 cob loaf

+

2 garlic cloves

+

A few sprigs parsley

Fry over medium heat

3 MINUTES

Cut in a grid pattern without touching the bottom

Insert between cuts

+

400 g (14 oz) crushed tomatoes

+

150 g (5⅓ oz) comté or Gruyère cheese

Bake at 180°C (350°F)

20 MINUTES

SERVES 4
PREPARATION: 10 MINUTES
COOKING: 28 MINUTES

- 250 g (9 oz) button mushrooms, sliced
- 2 tablespoons olive oil
- 1 cob loaf
- 2 garlic cloves, crushed
- a few sprigs parsley, chopped
- salt and pepper to taste
- 400 g (14 oz) crushed tomatoes
- 150 g (5⅓ oz) comté or Gruyère cheese, grated

146 AVOCADO
roses
—

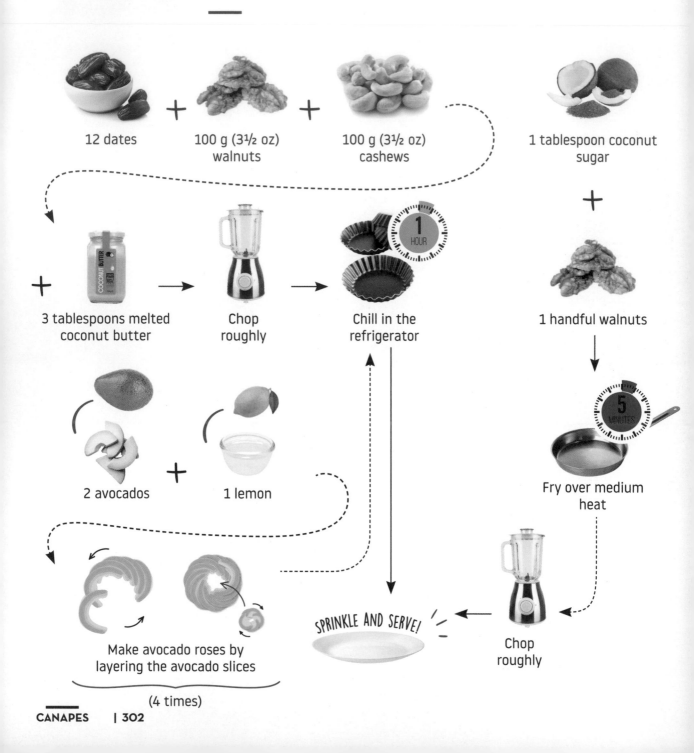

12 dates + 100 g (3½ oz) walnuts + 100 g (3½ oz) cashews

1 tablespoon coconut sugar

+ 3 tablespoons melted coconut butter → Chop roughly → Chill in the refrigerator

1 HOUR

+

1 handful walnuts

2 avocados + 1 lemon

5 MINUTES

Fry over medium heat

Make avocado roses by layering the avocado slices

(4 times)

SPRINKLE AND SERVE!

Chop roughly

SERVES 4
PREPARATION: 15 MINUTES
RESTING: 1 HOUR
COOKING: 5 MINUTES

- 12 dates, pitted
- 100 g (3½ oz) walnuts
  + a handful
- 100 g (3½ oz) cashews
- 3 tablespoons coconut butter
- 1 tablespoon coconut sugar
- 2 avocados, peeled, seeded
  and sliced
- 1 lemon, juiced

147 FRUITY
rice paper rolls

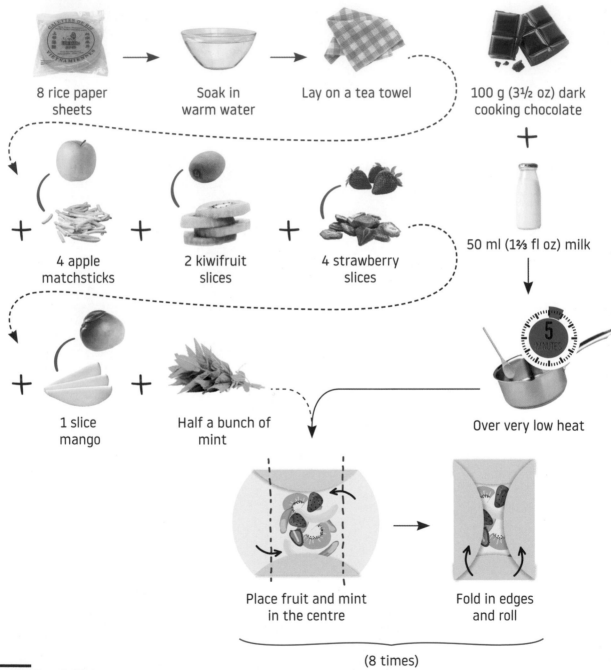

8 rice paper sheets

Soak in warm water

Lay on a tea towel

100 g (3½ oz) dark cooking chocolate

+

4 apple matchsticks

+

2 kiwifruit slices

+

4 strawberry slices

50 ml (1⅔ fl oz) milk

+

1 slice mango

+

Half a bunch of mint

5 MINUTES

Over very low heat

Place fruit and mint in the centre

Fold in edges and roll

(8 times)

MAKES 8 ROLLS
PREPARATION: 10 MINUTES
COOKING: 5 MINUTES

- 8 rice paper sheets
- 100 g (3½ oz) dark cooking chocolate
- 50 ml (1⅔ fl oz) milk
- 1 apple, cut into match sticks
- 2 kiwifruit, sliced
- 1 punnet strawberries, hulled and sliced
- 1 mango, peeled and cut into pieces
- ½ bunch mint

148 SUMMER
fruit skewers
—

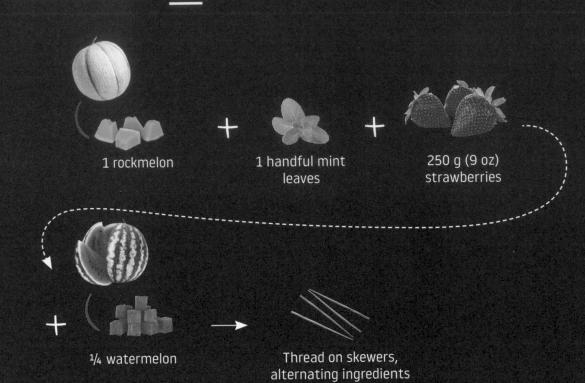

1 rockmelon + 1 handful mint leaves + 250 g (9 oz) strawberries

+ ¼ watermelon → Thread on skewers, alternating ingredients

SERVES 4
PREPARATION: 15 MINUTES

- 1 rockmelon, peeled and cut into pieces
- 1 handful mint leaves
- 250 g (9 oz) strawberries
- ¼ watermelon, rind removed and cut into pieces

149 CARAMEL
strawberries

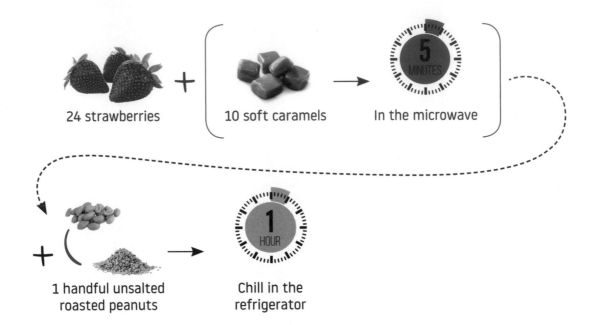

24 strawberries + 10 soft caramels → 5 MINUTES In the microwave

+ 1 handful unsalted roasted peanuts → 1 HOUR Chill in the refrigerator

SERVES 6
PREPARATION: 15 MINUTES
COOKING: 5 MINUTES
REFRIGERATOR: 1 HOUR

- 24 strawberries
- 10 soft caramels, melted
- 1 handful unsalted roasted peanuts, chopped

150 GRILLED PINEAPPLE
skewers

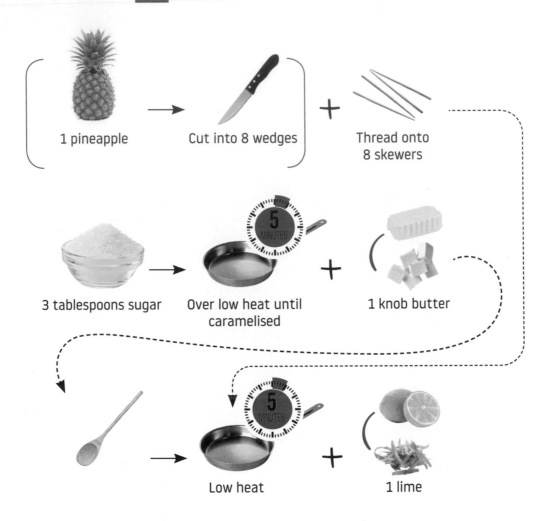

1 pineapple → Cut into 8 wedges + Thread onto 8 skewers

3 tablespoons sugar → Over low heat until caramelised (5 MINUTES) + 1 knob butter

Low heat (5 MINUTES) + 1 lime

SERVES 8
PREPARATION: 15 MINUTES
COOKING: 10 MINUTES

- 1 pineapple, peeled and cut into 8 wedges
- 3 tablespoons sugar
- 1 knob butter
- 1 lime, zested

COCKTAIL INDEX BY ALCOHOL

RECIPE INDEX BY OTHER INGREDIENTS

A Gelding Street Press book
An Imprint of Rockpool Publishing, Pty Ltd.
PO Box 252, Summer Hill
NSW 2130, Australia

www.geldingstreetpress.com
Follow us! @ geldingstreet_press

Originally published in French by Larousse as *Cocktails et Apéritifs Sans Bla Bla*
under ISBN: 9782036028210 © Larousse 2021

This edition published in 2024 by Gelding Street Press
ISBN: 9780645207156

RECIPE CREDITS © LAROUSSE

Vincent Amiel: 07, 51; Séverine Augé: 04, 92; Anna Austry: 114, 121, 135, 142; Blandine Boyer: 129, 136; Déborah Charlemoine: 14, 18, 33, 36, 37, 38, 47, 55, 70, 85, 86; Catherine Conan: 118, 131, 132; Audrey Cosson: 111, 112, 123, 147; Valéry Drouet: 53; Marine Durand: 113, 146; Coralie Ferreira: 109, 140, 141, 143; Matthias Giroud: 54, 84; Guillaume Guerbois: 08, 12, 14, 18, 28, 33, 34, 36, 37, 38, 44, 46, 47, 49, 50, 55, 56, 57, 60, 61, 64, 65, 67, 68, 70, 85, 86, 94, 100, 108; Isabelle Guerre: 145; Sandrine Houdré-Grégoire: 02, 03, 05, 10, 11, 13, 15, 16, 17, 20, 21, 25, 27, 28, 29, 30, 31, 32, 35, 39, 42, 43, 45, 46, 48, 50, 54, 58, 59, 61, 63, 64, 65, 67, 68, 69, 71, 72, 73, 74, 75, 76, 79, 80, 81, 82, 83, 84, 87, 88, 89, 91, 93, 94, 95, 96, 97, 98, 99, 100, 101, 102, 103, 104, 105, 106, 107, 108; Béatrice Lagandré: 119; Delphine Lebrun: 116, 126; Anne Loiseau: 90, 110; Mélanie Martin: 125, 133, 137; Quitterie Pasquesoone: 117, 144; Sylvie Rost: 78; Aude Royer: 115, 148; Julie Soucail: 128; Noémie Strouk: 120, 124, 127, 130, 134, 138, 139, 149, 150.

PHOTOGRAPHY CREDITS © LAROUSSE

Fabrice Besse: 02, 03, 08, 12, 13, 15, 16, 25, 27, 29, 34, 35, 39, 44, 48, 49, 56, 57, 59, 60, 69, 74, 75, 76, 79, 80, 81, 82, 83, 87, 89, 98, 99, 104, 122, 148; David Bonnier: 127, 134; Aimery Road: 109, 140, 141, 143; Emanuela Cino: 10, 11, 20, 42, 58, 91, 110, 115, 133, 137; Delphine Constantini: P.10–11, 07, 11, 51, 118, 131, 132; Charly Deslandes: 04, 14, 17, 18, 21, 22, 28, 30, 32, 33, 36, 37, 38, 43, 45, 46, 47, 50, 55, 61, 64, 65, 67, 68, 70, 71, 72, 73, 85, 86, 88, 92, 93, 94, 95, 96, 97, 100, 101, 102, 103, 105, 106, 107, 108; Loran Dhérines: 01, 54; Sophie Dumont: 114, 116, 121, 126, 142; Virginie Garnier: 111, 112, 123, 147; Amandine Honegger: 78, 117, 119, 129, 136, 144; Marie-José Jarry: 05, 84; Anne Loiseau: 90; Céline Mermet-Bouvier: 135; Olivier Ploton: 63, 120, 124, 130, 138, 139, 149, 150; Aline Princet: 125, 145; Fabrice Veigas: 113, 128, 146; Pierre-Louis Viel: 53

PHOTOGRAPHY CREDITS © SHUTTERSTOCK

Cover, Cavan Images: 32; Vladislav Chusov: 09; Yuli Furman: 66; Lukas Gojda: 19; Grafvision: 23; Mateusz Gzik: 52; Brent Hofacker: 06, 40; Evgeny Karandaev: 41; Olexander Kozak: 62; Ivan Mateev: 24 Salivanchuk Semen: 26; Vasanty: 77

CREDITS PHOTOS AND DRAWINGS OF INGREDIENTS AND UTENSILS

© Shutterstock, © Thinkstock.

A NOTE ABOUT THE MEASUREMENTS

Please note that these recipes use 15 ml tablespoon measures.
1 tablespoon = 15 ml/½ fl oz/3 teaspoons

Cover design by Alissa Dinallo

Printed and bound in China
10 9 8 7 6 5 4 3 2 1